Joseph Alexander Altsheler

The Sun of Saratoga

A Romance of Burgoyne's Surrender

Joseph Alexander Altsheler

The Sun of Saratoga
A Romance of Burgoyne's Surrender

ISBN/EAN: 9783744723688

Printed in Europe, USA, Canada, Australia, Japan

Cover: Foto ©Thomas Meinert / pixelio.de

More available books at **www.hansebooks.com**

THE SUN
OF SARATOGA

A Romance of Burgoyne's Surrender

BY

JOSEPH A. ALTSHELER

NEW YORK
D. APPLETON AND COMPANY
1897

CONTENTS.

THE SUN OF SARATOGA.

CHAPTER I.

ON WATCH.

"You will watch this hollow and the hill yonder," said the general, "and see that not a soul passes either to the north or to the south. Don't forget that the fate of all the colonies may depend upon your vigilance."

Then he left me.

I felt much discomfort. I submit that it is not cheering to have the fate of thirteen large colonies and some two or three million people, men, women, and children, depend upon one's own humble self. I like importance, but not when it brings such an excess of care.

I looked to Sergeant Whitestone for cheer.

"We are not the only men on watch to cut off their messengers," he said. "We have our bit of ground here to guard, and others have theirs."

Then he sat down on the turf and smoked
his pipe with provoking calm, as if the troubles
of other people were sufficient to take our own
away. I decided to stop thinking about failure
and address myself to my task. Leaving the
sergeant and the four men who constituted
my small army, I took a look about me. The
hollow was but a few hundred yards across,
sparse-set with trees and bushes. It should not
be difficult to guard it by day, but by night
it would be a different matter. On the hill
I could see the walls and roof of the Van Auken house. That, too, fell within my terri-
tory, and for reasons sufficient to me I was sorry
of it.

I walked part of the way up the hillside,
spying out the ground and seeing what places
for concealment there might be. I did not
mean to be lax in my duty in any particular.
I appreciated its full import. The great idea
that we might take Burgoyne and his whole
army was spreading among us, and it was
vital that no news of his plight should
reach Clinton and the other British down
below us.

I came back to Sergeant Whitestone, who

was still sitting on the ground, puffing out much smoke, and looking very content.

"I don't think we need fear any attempt to get through until night," he said. "The dark is the time for messengers who don't want to be seen."

I agreed with him, and found a position of comfort upon the grass.

"There's our weak point," said the sergeant, waving his hand toward the Van Auken house.

I was sorry to hear him say so, especially as I had formed the same opinion.

"But there's nobody up there except women," I said.

"The very reason," replied the sergeant.

I occupied myself for a little while tossing pebbles at a tree. Then I disposed my men at suitable distances along our line, and concluded to go up to the house, which going, in good truth, was part of my duty.

I was near the top of the hill when I saw Kate Van Auken coming to meet me.

"Good morning, Dick," she said.

"Good morning, Mistress Catherine," I replied.

It had been my habit to call her Kate when we were children together, but I could not quite manage it now.

"You are set as a guard upon us?" she said.

"To protect you from harm," I replied with my most gallant air.

"Your manners are improving," she said in what I thought rather a disdainful tone.

"I must search the house," I continued.

"You call that protecting us?" she said with the same touch of sarcasm.

"Nevertheless it must be done," I said, speaking in my most positive manner.

She led the way without further demur. Now I had every confidence in Kate Van Auken. I considered her as good a patriot as myself, though all her family were Tory. It did not seem to me to be at all likely that any spy or messenger of the British had reached the concealment of the house, but it was my duty to be sure.

"Perhaps you would not care to talk to my mother?" she asked.

"No!" I replied in such haste that she laughed.

I knew Madame Van Auken was one of the

most fanatic Tories in New York colony, and I had no mind to face her. It is curious how women are more hard-set than men in these matters. But in my search of the house I was compelled to pass through the room where she sat, most haughty and severe. Kate explained what I was about. She never spoke to me, though she had known me since I was a baby, but remained rigid in her armchair and glowered at me as if I were a most wretched villain. I confess that I felt very uncomfortable, and was glad when we passed on to another room.

As I had expected, I found nothing suspicious in the house.

" I hope you are satisfied? " said Miss Van Auken when I left.

" For the present," I replied, bowing.

I rejoined Sergeant Whitestone in the hollow. He was still puffing at his pipe, and I do not think he had changed his position by the breadth of a hair. I told him I had found nothing at the house, and asked what he thought of the case.

" We may look for work to-night, I think," he replied very gravely. " It's most likely that the British will try to send somebody through at this point. All the Van Aukens, except the women, are with Burgoyne, and as they know the ground around here best they'll go to Burgoyne and have him send the men this way."

That was my thought too. Whitestone is a man of sound judgment. I sent two of our lads toward the house, with instructions to watch it, front and rear. It was my intent to visit them there later.

Then I joined Whitestone in a friendly pipe and found much consolation in the good tobacco. Kate's manner had nettled me the least bit, but I reflected that perhaps she was justified, as so many of her people were with Burgoyne, and, moreover, she was betrothed to Chudleigh, an Englishman. Chudleigh, an officer with Tryon in New York before the war, had come down from Canada with Burgoyne. So far as I knew he had passed safely through the last battle.

I had naught in particular against Chudleigh, but it seemed to me that he might find a wife in his own country.

The day was slow. I would rather have been with the army, where there was bustle and the hope of great things, but Whitestone, a pack of lazy bones, grunted with content. He stretched his long body on the ground and stared up at the sky through half-closed eyes. A mellow sun shone back at him.

Toward noon I sent one of the men to the house with a request for some small supply of provision, if they could spare it. We had food, a little, but we wanted more. Perhaps I ought to have gone myself, but I had my reasons. The man came back with two roast chickens.

" The old lady gave me a blessing," he said with a sour face, " and said she'd die before she'd feed rebels against the best king that ever lived; but the girl gave me these when I came out the back way."

We ate our dinner, and then I changed the sentinels at the house. Whitestone relapsed into his apparent lethargy, but I knew that the man, despite his seeming, was all vigilance and caution.

We looked for no happenings before dark, but it was yet a good four hours to set of sun when we heard a noise in the south and saw some dust rising far down the hollow.

Sergeant Whitestone rose quickly to his feet, smothered the fire in his pipe, and put his beloved companion in an inside pocket of his waistcoat.

"A party coming," I said.

"Yes, and a lot of 'em, too, I think," he replied, "or they wouldn't raise so much dust."

One of the men ran down from the hill where the view was better, and announced that a large body of soldiers was approaching. I called all the others and we stood to our arms, though we were convinced that the men marching were our own. Either the British would come with a great army or not at all.

The approaching troops, two hundred at least, appeared down the valley. The dust encased them like armor, and one can not tell what a soldier is by the dirt on his uniform. Whitestone took one long and critical look and then unbuttoned his coat and drew out his pipe.

"What are they?" I asked.

"Virginians," he replied. "I know their stride. I've served with 'em. Each step they take is exactly two inches longer than ours. They got it hunting 'possums at night."

They were in loose order like men who have marched far, but their faces were eager, and they were well armed. We halted them, as our duty bade us, and asked who they were.

"Re-enforcements for the Northern army," said the captain at their head. He showed us an order from our great commander-in-chief himself.

"Where is Burgoyne?" he asked as soon as I had finished the letter. "Is he still coming south?"

"He is but a few miles beyond you," I replied, "and he will come no farther south. There has been a great battle and we held him fast."

They gave a cheer, and some threw up their hats. To understand our feelings one must remember that we had been very near the edge of the ice, and more than once thought we would go over.

All their weariness gone, these long-legged Southerners shouldered their rifles and marched on to join the great belt of strong arms and stout hearts that was forming around the doomed Burgoyne and his army. As they passed, Sergeant Whitestone took his pipe out of his mouth and said:

"Good boys!"

Which was short, but which was much for him.

I watched their dusty backs as they tramped up the valley.

"You seem to admire them," said some one over my shoulder.

"It is they and their fellows who will take Burgoyne, Mistress Catherine," I replied.

"They can't stand before the British bayonet," she said.

"Sorry to dispute the word of so fair a lady," I replied, meaning to be gallant, "but I was at the last battle."

She laughed, as if she did not think much of my words. She said no more, but watched the marching Virginians. I thought I saw a little glow as of pride come in her face. They curved around a hill and passed out of sight.

"Good-by!" said Mistress Kate. "That's all I wanted to see here."

She went back to the house and we resumed our tedious watch. Whitestone had full warrant for his seeming apathy. After the passage of the Virginians there was naught to stir us in the slightest. Though born and bred a country-man, I have never seen anything more quiet and peaceful than that afternoon, although two large armies lay but a short distance away, resting from one bloody battle and waiting for another.

No one moved at the house. Everybody seemed to be asleep there. Some birds chattered undisturbed in the trees. The air had the crisp touch of early autumn, and faint tokens of changing hues were appearing already in the foliage. I felt a sleepy languor like that which early spring puts into the blood. In order to shake it off I began a thorough search of the country thereabouts. I pushed my way through the bushes, and tramped both to the north and to the south as far as I dared go from my post. Then I visited the guards who adjoined my little detachment on either side. They had to report only the same calm that prevailed at our part of the line. I went back to Sergeant Whitestone.

" Better take it easy," advised he. " When there's nothing to do, do it, and then be fresh to do it when there's something to do."

I took his advice, which seemed good, and again made myself comfortable on the ground, waiting for the coming of the night. It was still

an hour to set of sun when we saw a mounted
officer coming from the north where our army
lay. We seemed to be his destination, as he rode
straight-toward us. I recognized Captain Martyn at once. I did not like this man. I had no
particular reason for it, though I have found
often that the lack of reason for doing a thing
is the very strongest reason why we do it. I
knew little about Captain Martyn. He had
joined the Northern army before I arrived, and
they said he had done good service, especially
in the way of procuring information about the
enemy.

Whitestone and I sat together on the grass.
The other men were on guard at various points.
Captain Martyn came on at a good pace until
he reached us, when he pulled up his horse with
a smart jerk.

" Your watch is over," he said to me without preliminary. " You are to withdraw with
your men at once."

I was taken much aback, as any one else in
my place would have been also. I had received
instructions to keep faithful guard over that
portion of the line for the long period of twenty-
four hours—that is, until the next morning.

"But this must be a mistake," I protested. "There is nobody to relieve us. Surely the general can not mean to leave the line broken at this point."

"If you have taken the direction of the campaign, perhaps you had best notify our generals that they are superseded," he said in a tone most ironical.

He aroused my stubbornness, of which some people say I have too much, and I refused to retire until he showed me a written order to that effect from the proper officer. Not abating his ironical manner one whit, he held it toward me in an indifferent way, as much as to say, "You can read it or not, just as you choose; it does not matter to me."

It was addressed to me, and notified me briefly to withdraw at once with my men and rejoin my company, stationed not less than ten miles away. Everything, signature included, was most proper, and naught was left for me to do but to obey. The change was no affair of mine.

"Does that put your mind at rest?" asked Martyn.

"No, it does not," I replied, "but it takes responsibility from me."

Sergeant Whitestone called the men, and as we marched over the hill Martyn turned his horse and galloped back toward the army. When he had passed out of sight behind the trees I ordered the men to stop.

"Whitestone," said I to the sergeant, who, as I have said before, was a man of most acute judgment, "do you like this?"

"Small liking have I for it," he replied. "It is the most unmilitary proceeding I ever knew. It may be that our relief is coming, but it should have arrived before we left."

I took out the order again, and after scanning it with care passed it to White-stone.

Neither of us could see anything wrong with it. But the sergeant's manner confirmed me in a resolution I had taken before I put the question to him.

"Sergeant," I said, "every man in our army knows of what great import it is that no messenger from the British should get through our lines. We are leaving unguarded a place wide enough for a whole company to pass. I think

I'll go back there and resume guard. Will you go with me?"

He assented with most cheerful alacrity, and when I put the question to the others, stating that I left them to do as they pleased, all joined me. For what they believed to be the good of the cause they were willing to take the risks of disobedience, and I was proud of them.

I looked about me from the crest of the hill, but Martyn was out of sight. We returned to the valley and I posted my men in the same positions as before, my forebodings that it would be a night of action increased by this event.

CHAPTER II.

Two of my men were stationed near the house, but I had so placed them that they could not be seen by any one inside. I had also concealed our return from possible watchers there. I had an idea, which I confided to Whitestone, and in which, with his usual sound sense, he agreed with me. He and I remained together in the valley and watched the night come.

The sun seemed to me to linger long at the edge of the far hills, but at last his red rim went out of sight, and the heavy darkness which precedes the moonlight fell upon the earth.

" If anything happens, it will happen soon," said Whitestone.

That was obvious, because if Martyn meditated treachery, it would be important for him to carry it out before the unguarded point in the line was discovered. Officially it was unguarded, because we were supposed to have gone away and stayed away.

My suspicions were confirmed by the non-arrival of our relief. Whitestone still took his ease, stretched out on the ground in the valley. I knew he missed his pipe, but to light it would serve as a warning in the dark to any one. I visited the two men near the house and cautioned them to relax their watch in no particular.

The night was now well begun and I could see no great distance. As I turned away from the last man I chanced to look up at the house, whose shape was but a darker shadow in the darkness. At a narrow window high up, where the sloping eaves converged, I saw a light. Perhaps I would not have thought much of it, but the light was moved from side to side with what seemed to me to be regular and deliberate motion. It faced the north, where our army lay.

I walked twenty steps or so, still keeping the light in view. Its regular swinging motion from side to side did not cease, and I could not persuade myself that it was not intended as a signal to some one. The discovery caused in me a certain faintness at the heart, for until this night I had thought Kate Van Auken, despite mother, brother, and all else, was a true friend to our cause through all.

I own I was in great perplexity. At first I was tempted to enter the house, smash the light, and denounce her in my most eloquent language. But I quickly saw the idea was but folly, and would stand in the way of our own plans. I leaned against an oak tree and kept my eyes fixed on the light. Though the windows in the house were many, no other light was visible, which seemed strange to me, for it was very early. Back and forth it swung, and then it was gone with a suddenness which made me rub my eyes to see if it were not still there; nothing ailed them. The building was a huge black shadow, but no light shone from it anywhere.

I went in a mighty hurry to Whitestone and told him what I had seen. He loosened the pistol in his belt and said he thought the time for us to make discoveries had come. Once more I agreed with him.

I drew my own pistol, that it might be ready to my hand, if need be, and we walked a bit up the valley. It was very dark and we trusted more to our ears than to our eyes, in which trust we were not deceived, for speedily we heard a faint but regular thump, thump, upon the earth.

"A horse coming," I said. ·

"And probably a horseman, too," said Whitestone.

How glad was I that we had stayed! It was not at all likely that the man coming had any honest business there. We stepped a trifle to one side and stood silent, while the tread of the horse's hoofs grew louder. In a few moments the horseman was near enough for us to see his face even in the night, and I felt no surprise, though much anger, when I recognized Captain Martyn. He was riding slowly, in order that he might not make much noise, I supposed.

I stepped forward and put my hand upon his bridle rein. He saw who it was and uttered an exclamation; but after that he recovered his self-control with a quickness most astonishing.

"How dare you stop me in such a sudden and alarming manner?" he said with an appearance of great wrath.

But, very sure now that I was right, I intended neither to be deceived nor overborne. I ordered him to dismount and surrender himself.

" You are very impertinent, sir," he said, " and need chastisement."

I told him it mattered not, and ordered him again to dismount. For reply he drew a pistol with such suddenness that I could not guard against it and fired point-blank at my face. It was the kindly darkness making his aim bad that saved me. The bullet passed me, but the smoke and flash blinded me.

The traitor lashed his horse in an attempt to gallop by us, but Whitestone also fired, his bullet striking the horse and not the man. The animal, in pain, reared and struck out with his feet. Martyn attempted to urge him forward but failed. Then he slipped from his back and ran into the bushes. My eyes were clear now, and Whitestone and I rushed after him.

I noted from the very first that the man ran toward the house, and again, even in that moment of excitement, I congratulated myself that I had expected treason and collusion and had come back to my post.

I saw the captain's head appearing just above some of the short bushes and raised my pistol to fire at him, but before I could get the proper aim he was out of sight. We increased our efforts in fear lest we should lose him, and a few steps further heard a shot which I knew came from one of my men on guard. We met the man running toward us, his empty rifle in his hand. He told us the fugitive had turned the corner of the house, and I felt that we had trapped him then, for the second man on guard there would be sure to stop him.

We pressed forward and met the man from behind the house, attracted by the sound of shots. He said nobody had appeared there. I turned to a side door, convinced that Martyn had found refuge in the house. It was no time to stand upon courtesy, or to wait for an invitation to enter. The door was locked, but Whitestone and I threw our full weight against it at the same time, and it flew open under the impact of some twenty-five stone.

We fell into a dark hall and scrambled in pressing haste to our feet. I paused a moment that I might direct the soldiers to surround the house and seize any one who came forth. Then we turned to face Madame Van Auken, who was coming toward us, a candle in her hand, a long white robe around her person, and a most icy look on her face.

She began at once a very fierce attack upon us for disturbing quiet folks abed. I have ever stood in dread of woman's tongue, to which there is but seldom answer, but I explained in great hurry that a traitor had taken refuge in her house, and search it again we must, if not with her consent, then without it. She repelled me with extreme haughtiness, saying such conduct was unworthy of men who pretended to breeding; but, after all, it was no more than she ought to expect from ungrateful rebels.

Her attack, most unwarranted, considering the fact that a traitor had just hid in her house, stirred some spleen in me, and I bade her very stiffly to stand out of the way. Another light appeared just then at the head of the stairway, and Mistress Kate came down, fully dressed, looking very fine and handsome too, with a red flame in either cheek.

She demanded the reason of our entry with a degree of haughtiness inferior in no wise to her mother's. Again I explained, angered at these delays made by women who, handsome or not, may appear sometimes when they are not wanted.

"Take the men, all except one to watch at the door, and search the house at once, sergeant," said I.

Whitestone, with an indifference to their bitter words most astonishing, led his men upstairs and left me to endure it all. I pretended not to hear, and taking the candle suddenly from Kate's hands turned into a side room and began to poke about the furniture. But they followed me there.

"I suppose you think this is very shrewd and very noble," said Kate with a fine irony.

I did not reply, but poked behind a sideboard with my pistol muzzle. Both Kate and her mother seemed to me, despite their efforts to repress it, to manifest a very great uneasiness. I did not wonder at it, for I knew they must fear to be detected in their collusion with the traitor. Kate continued to gibe at me.

"Oh, well, it's not Captain Chudleigh I'm looking for," said I at last.

"And in truth if it were, you'd be afraid

to find him," replied she, a sprightly flash appearing in her eye.

I said no more, content with my hit. I found no one below stairs, and joined Whitestone on the second floor, the women still following me and upbraiding me. I looked more than once at Kate, and I could see that she was all in a tremor. I doubted not it arose from a belief that I had discovered her treachery, as well as from a fear that we would capture the chief traitor.

Whitestone had not yet found our man, though he had been in every room on the second floor and even into the low-roofed garret. At this the two women became more contumelious, crying out that we were now shamed by our own acts. But we were confident that the man was yet in the house. I pushed into a large room which seemed to serve as a spare chamber. We had entered it once before, but I thought a more thorough search might be made. In one corner, some dresses hanging against the wall reached to the floor. I prodded one of them with my fist and encountered something soft.

The dress was dashed aside and our man

sprang out. There was a low window at the
end of the room, and with one bound he was
through it. Whitestone fired at his disappearing body, but missed. We heard a second shot
from the man on guard below, and then we
rushed pell-mell down the stairs to pursue him.

I bethought me at the door to bid one of the
men stay and watch the house, for I knew not
what further treachery the women might medi-
tate. This stopped me only a moment, and
then I ran after Whitestone, who was some
steps in the lead. We overtook the man who
had fired at Martyn, and he said he had hit him,
so he thought.

" When he sprang from the window he rose
very 'light from the ground," he said, " and I
don't think the fall hurt him much."

We saw Martyn some twenty yards or more
in advance of us, running toward the south.
It was of double importance now that we should
overtake him, for if we did not he would be
beyond our lines, and, barring some improbable
chance, would escape to Clinton with a report
of Burgoyne's condition.

The fugitive curved here and there among
the shadows but could not shake us off.   I

held my loaded pistol in my hand and twice or thrice had a chance for a fair shot at him, but I never raised the weapon. I could shoot at a man in the heat of battle or the flurry of a sudden moment of excitement, but not when he was like a fleeing hare. Moreover, I preferred to take him alive.

The moon was coming out, driving away part of the darkness, and on the bushes I noticed some spots of blood. Then the fugitive had been hit, and I was glad I had not fired upon him, for we would be certain to take him wounded.

The course led over pretty rough ground. Whitestone was panting at my elbow, and two of the men lumbered behind us. The fugitive began to waver, and presently I noticed that we were gaining. Suddenly Martyn began to cast his hands as if he were throwing something from him, and we saw little bits of white paper fluttering in the air. I divined on the instant that, seeing his certain capture, he was tearing up traitorous papers. We wanted those papers as well as their bearer.

I shouted to him to halt lest I fire. He flung a whole handful of scraps from him. Just

then he came to a stump; he stopped abruptly,
sat down upon it with his face to us, and drawing a pistol from his pocket, put it to his own
head and fired.

I was never more shocked in my life, the
thing was so sudden. He slid off the stump to
the ground, and when we reached him he was
quite dead. We found no letters upon him,
as in the course of his flight he had succeeded in
destroying them all. But I had not the slightest doubt the order he had given to me would
soon prove to be a forgery. His own actions
had been sufficient evidence of that.

I directed Whitestone to take the body to
some safe place and we would give it quiet
burial on the morrow. I did not wish the
women to know of the man's terrible fate,
though I owed them scant courtesy for the way
they had treated me.

Leaving Whitestone and one of the soldiers
to the task, I went back to the house alone.

Mistress Kate and her mother were at the
door, both in a state of high excitement.

" Did he escape? " asked Madame Van
Auken.

" No," I replied, telling the truth in part

3

and a lie in part. " We captured him, and the men are now taking him back to the army."

She sighed deeply. Mistress Kate said nothing, though her face was of a great paleness.

" I will not upbraid you with what I call treachery," I said, speaking to them both, " and I will not disturb you again to-night. It is not necessary."

I said the last rather grimly, but I observed some of the paleness depart from Mistress Kate's countenance and a look strangely like that of relief come into her eyes. I was sorry, for it seemed to me to indicate more thought of her own and her mother's peace than of the fate of the man whom we had taken. But there was naught to say, and I left them without the courtesy of a good night on either side.

Whitestone and the men returned presently from their task, and I posted the guards as before, confident that no traitor could pass while I was on watch there.

CHAPTER III.

Whitestone and I held a small conference in the dark. Though regretting that the matter had ended in such tragic way, we believed we had done a great thing, and I am not loath to confess that I expected words of approval the next day when we would take the news of it to the army. We agreed that we must not relax our vigilance in the smallest particular, for where there was one plot there might be a dozen. Whitestone went down into the valley while I remained near the house.

In my lonely watch I had great space for thought. I was grieved by my discoveries in regard to Kate Van Auken. Of a truth she was nothing to me, being betrothed, moreover, to Chudleigh the Englishman; but we had been children together, and it was not pleasing to believe her a patriot and find her a traitor. I

29

could get no sort of satisfaction out of such thoughts, and turning them aside walked about with vigor in an attempt to keep myself from becoming very sleepy.

The moon was still showing herself, and I could see the house very well. No light had appeared in it since our last withdrawal, but looking very closely I saw what appeared to be a dark shadow at one of the windows. I knew that room to be Mistress Kate's, and I surmised that she was there seeking to watch us. I resolved in return that I would watch her. I stepped back where I would be sheltered by a tree from her sight, and presently had my reward. The window was opened gently and a head, which could be none other than that of Kate, was thrust out a bit.

I could see her quite well, even the features of her face. She was looking very earnestly into the surrounding night, and of a truth anxiety was writ plainly on her countenance. She stretched her head out farther and examined all the space before the house. I was hidden from her gaze, but down in a corner of the yard she could see the sentinel pacing back and forth. She inspected him with much earnestness for some time, and then withdrew her head, closing the window.

I was of the opinion that some further mischief was afoot or intended, but the nature of it passed me. It seemed that what had happened already was not a sufficient warning to them. I began to walk around the house that I might keep a watch upon it from every point. Sleepiness no longer oppressed me. In truth, I forgot all about it.

I passed to the rear of the building and spoke to the sentinel stationed in the yard there. He had seen nothing of suspicious nature so far. I knew he was a faithful, watchful man, and that I could trust him. I left him and pushed my way between two large flower bushes growing very close together. Standing there, I beheld the opening of another window in the house. Again the head of Mistress Kate appeared, and precisely the same act as before was repeated. She looked about with the intentness and anxiety of a military engineer studying his ground. She saw the sentinel as she had seen his fellow before the house, and her eyes rested long upon him. Her examination finished, she withdrew, closing the window.

I set myself to deciphering the meaning of this, and of a sudden it flashed upon me with such force that I believed myself stupid not to have seen it before. Kate Van Auken herself was planning to go through our lines with the news of Burgoyne's plight. She was a bold girl, not much afraid of the dark or the woods, and the venture was not beyond her. The conviction of the truth depressed me. I felt some regard for Kate Van Auken, whom I as a little boy had liked as a little girl, and I had slight relish for this task of keeping watch upon her. Even now I had caught her planning great harm to our cause.

I confess that I scarce knew what to do. Perhaps it was my duty, if the matter be considered in its utmost strictness, to arrest both the women at once as dangerous to our cause, and send them to the army. But such a course was quite beyond my resolution. I could not do it. Being unable to decide upon anything else, I continued my watch, determined that Mistress Kate should not escape from the house.

The moon withdrew herself and then there was an increase of darkness. Again I was thankful that I had been vigilant, for I saw a small door in the rear of the house open. I could not doubt that it opened to let forth Catherine Van Auken upon her traitorous errand. I made my resolution upon the instant. If she came out, I would seize her and compel her to return to the house in all quiet, in order that Whitestone and the others might not know.

My suspicions—my fears, in truth I may call them—were justified, for in a few moments her well-known figure appeared in the doorway all clothed about in a great dark cloak and hood, like one preparing for a long night's journey. I retreated a little, for it was my purpose to draw her on and then catch her, when no doubt about her errand could arise.

She stood in the doorway for perhaps two minutes repeating her actions at the window; that is, she looked around carefully to note how we were watching. I could not see her face owing to the increase of darkness and her attitude, but I had no doubt the same anxiety and eagerness were writ there.

Presently she seemed to arrange her dark draperies in a manner more satisfactory and, stooping somewhat, came out of the house.

The sentinel in this part of the yard was doing his duty and was as watchful as could be, but he could scarce see this shadow gliding along in the larger shadow of the rose bushes. I deemed it good fortune that I was there to see and prevent the flight. I would face her and confound her with the proof of her guilt.

She came on quite rapidly, and I shrank a little farther back into the rose bushes. Her course was directly toward me, and suddenly I rose up in the path. I expected her to show great surprise and to cry out after the fashion of women, but she did not. In truth I fancied I saw a start, but that was all. In a moment she whirled about and fled back toward the house with as little noise as the shadow she resembled. I had scarce recovered my presence of mind when she was halfway to the house, but I pursued in the effort to overtake her and confound her.

I observed that when she came forth she had shut the door behind her, but as she fled swiftly back it seemed to open of its own accord for her entrance. She passed within, disappearing like a ghost, and the door was shut with a snap almost in my face. I put my hands upon it and found it was very real and substantial—perhaps a stout two inches in thickness.

I deliberated with myself for a moment or two and concluded to do nothing further in the matter. Perhaps it had turned out as well as might be, for I had stopped her errand, and her return, doubtless, had released me from unpleasant necessities.

I made no effort to force the door or to enter the house otherwise, but visited the sentinels, telling them to be of good caution, though I gave them no hint of what had happened.

I found Whitestone in the valley sitting on a stump and sucking at his pipe, which contained neither fire nor tobacco. He told me naught unusual had happened there. I took him back to the house with me, and together we watched about it until the coming of the day, without further event of interest.

Sunrise found my men and me very tired and sleepy, as we had a right to be, having been on guard near to twenty-four hours, with some very exciting things occurring in that long space. I awaited the relief which must come soon, for we were not iron men.

The sun had scarce swung clear of the earth when a door of the house was opened and Mistress Kate coming out, a pail in hand, walked lightly toward the well. I approached her, and she greeted me with an unconcern that amazed me.

" I trust that you enjoyed your night watch, Master Shelby? " she said.

" As well as was likely under the circumstances," I replied. " I hope that you slept soundly? "

" Nothing disturbed us after your invasion of our house," she said with fine calmness. " Now, will you help me draw this water? Since the approach of the armies there is no one left in the house save my mother and myself, and we must cook and do for ourselves."

I helped draw the water, and even carried the filled pail to the house for her, though she dismissed me at the door. But she atoned partly for her scant courtesy by bringing us a little later some loaves of white bread, which she said she had baked with her own hands, and which we found to be very good.

We had but finished breakfast when the soldiers who were to relieve us came, and right glad were we to see them.. They were followed a few minutes later by the colonel in charge, to whom I related the affair of Captain Martyn, and to whom I showed the order commanding us to withdraw. He instantly pronounced it a forgery and commended us for staying.

"It was a traitorous attempt to get through our line," he said, "but we are none the worse off, for it has failed."

I said nothing of Kate Van Auken's share in the conspiracy, but I told him the women in the house inclined strongly to the Tory side.

"I will see that the house is watched every moment of the day and night," he said.

Then I felt easy in mind and went off to sleep.

When I awoke it was about two by the sun, and the afternoon was fine. I heard that fresh troops had arrived from the Massachusetts and New Hampshire provinces in the morning, and the trap was closing down on Burgoyne tighter than ever. Everybody said another great battle was coming, and coming soon. Even then I heard the pop-pop of distant skirmishing and saw an occasional red flash on the horizon.

I was eager to be at the front, but such duty

was not for me then. As soon as I had eaten I was sent back with Sergeant Whitestone and the same men to keep watch at precisely the same point.

"Best take it easy," said the sergeant consolingly. "If the big battle's fought while we're away we can't get killed in it."

Then he lighted the inevitable pipe, smoked, and was content.

I questioned very closely the men whom we relieved near the house, and they said there had been nothing to note. The elder woman had never come out of the house, but the younger had been seen in the yard several times, though she had naught to say, and seemed to be concerned not at all about anything.

I thought it best not to visit the house, and took my station with Whitestone in the valley, disposing the men in much the same manner as before. Whitestone puffed at his pipe with the usual regularity and precision, but some of his taciturnity was gone. He was listening to the sounds of the skirmishing which came to us fitfully.

"The bees are stinging," said he. Then he added, with a fine mixture of metaphors: "The mouse is trying to feel his way out of the trap. The big battle can't be far off, for Burgoyne must know that every day lost is a chance lost."

It seemed to me that he was right, and I regretted more than ever my assignment to sentinel duty. I do not pretend to uncommon courage, but every soldier will bear me out that such waiting as we were doing is more trying than real battle.

Of a sudden the skirmishing seemed to take on an increase of vigor and to come nearer. Flashes appeared at various points on the horizon. Whitestone became deeply interested. He stood at his full height on a stump, and I would have done likewise had there been another stump. Presently he leaped down, exclaiming:

" I fancy there is work for us! "

I saw at once what he meant. A dozen men were coming down the valley at full speed. The bright sun even at the distance brought out the scarlet of their uniforms, and there was no mistaking the side to which they belonged. Evidently a party of Burgoyne's skirmishers had slipped through our main line somehow and

were bent upon escape southward, with all its
momentous consequences.

That escape we would prevent. I sent
Whitestone in a run to the two men near the
house to bid them take refuge behind it and
fight from its shelter. He was back in a breath,
and he and I and the other soldiers prepared to
hold the passage of the valley. Most fortunate
for us, a rail fence ran across this valley, and we
took refuge behind it—a wise precaution, I
think, since the approaching party outnumbered
us.

All of ours, except myself, had rifles, and I
carried two good pistols, with which I am no
bad shot. The British came on with much
speed. Two of them were mounted.

I glanced toward the house. At one of the
windows I saw a figure. I trusted if it was
Kate Van Auken that she would withdraw
speedily from such an exposed place. But I
had no time to note her presence further, for
just then the British seemed to perceive that
we barred the way, for they stopped as if hesitating. I suppose they saw us, as we were sheltered but in part by the fence.

Wishing to spare bloodshed I shouted to

them to surrender, but one of the men on horseback shook his head, said something to the
others, and they dashed toward us at all speed.
I recognized this man who appeared to be their
leader. He was Chudleigh, the Englishman,
the betrothed of Kate Van Auken, and, so far
as I knew, an honest, presentable fellow.

Whitestone poised his rifle on the top rail
of the fence and I surmised that it was aimed
at Chudleigh. Were the matter not so desperate I could have wished for a miss. But before
Whitestone pulled the trigger one of the men
from the shelter of the house fired, and Chudleigh's horse, struck by the ball intended for his
master, went down, tossing Chudleigh some distance upon the ground, where he lay quite still.
Whitestone transferred his aim and knocked
the other mounted man off his horse.

The remainder, not daunted by the warmth
of our greeting and the loss of their cavalry,
raised a cheer and rushed at us, firing their
pistols and muskets.

I do not scorn a skirmish. It may, and
often does, contain more heat to the square
yard than a great battle with twenty thousand
men engaged. These men bore down upon us

full of resolution. Their bullets pattered upon the rails of the fence, chipping off splinters. Some went between the rails and whizzed by us in fashion most uncomfortable. One man cried out a bit as the lead took him in the fleshy part of the leg, but he did not shrink from the onset.

Meanwhile we were not letting the time pass without profit, but fired at them with as much rapidity and aim as we could. The two men at the corner of the house helped us much with fine sharpshooting.

Our fortification, though but slender, gave us a great advantage, and nearly a third of their number had fallen before they were within a dozen feet of the fence. But it was our business not only to defeat them but to keep any from passing us. I was hopeful of doing this, for the sound of the firing had reached other portions of the line, and I saw re-enforcements for us coming on the run.

Our fire had been so hot that the British when within a dozen feet of us shrank back. Of a sudden one of them, a very active fellow, swerved to one side, darted at the fence, and leaping it with a single bound ran lightly along the hillside. I called to Whitestone and we followed him at all speed. I was confident that the others would be taken by our re-enforcements, who were coming up fast, and this man who had passed our line must be caught at all hazards.

One of my men at the house fired at the fugitive, but missed. My pistols were empty, and so was Whitestone's rifle. It was a matter which fleetness would decide and we made every effort.

The fugitive curved toward a wood back of the house, and we followed. I heard a rifle shot from a new direction, and Whitestone staggered; but in a moment he recovered himself, saying it was only a flesh wound. I was amazed, not at the shot but at the point from which it came. I looked up, and it was no mistake of hearing, for there was the white puff of smoke rising from an upper window in the house. It was but the glance of a moment, as the fugitive then claimed my attention. His speed was slackening and he seemed to be growing very tired.

A little blood appeared on Whitestone's arm near the shoulder, but he gave no other sign

4

that the wound affected him. Our man increased his speed a bit, but the effort exhausted
him; he stopped of a sudden, dropped to the
earth, and lay there panting, strength and
breath quite gone.

We ran up to him and demanded his surrender. He was too much exhausted to speak,
but he nodded as if he were glad the thing was
over. We let him rest until his breath came
back. Then he climbed to his feet, and, looking
at us, said in the fashion of one defending himself:

"I did the best I could; you can't say I
didn't."

"I guess you did," I replied. "You went
farther than any of your comrades."

He was a most likely young fellow, not more
than twenty, I should say, and I was very glad
he had come out of the affair unhurt. We took
him back to the valley, where the conflict was
over. Our re-enforcements had come up so fast
that the remainder of the British surrendered
after a few shots. All the prisoners were delivered to one of our captains who had arrived,
and he took them away. Then I turned my
attention to Whitestone. Having some small

knowledge of surgery, I asked him to let me see
his arm. He held it out without a word.

I pushed up his sleeve and found that the
bullet had cut only a little below the skin. I
bound up the scratch with a piece of old white
cloth, and said:

" You needn't bother about that, Whitestone; the bullet. that cut it wasn't very well
aimed."

" It was aimed pretty well, I think, for a
woman," he said.

"You won't say any more about that, Whitestone, will you? " I asked quietly.

" Not to anybody unless to you," he replied.

There was a faint smile on his face that I
did not altogether like; but he thrust his hand
into the inside pocket of his waistcoat, took
out his pipe, lighted the tobacco with great
deliberation, and began to smoke as if nothing
had happened.

The prisoners taken away and other signs of
conflict removed, we were left to our old duty,
and hill and hollow resumed their quiet. I was
much troubled, but at last I made up my mind
what to do. Asking Whitestone to keep a

good watch, I went to the house and knocked with much loudness at the front door. Kate opened the door, self-possessed and dignified.

"Miss Van Auken," I said with all my dignity, "I congratulate you upon your progress in the useful art of sharpshooting. You have wounded Sergeant Whitestone, a most excellent man, and perhaps it was chance only that saved him from death."

"Why should you blame me?" she said. "I wished the man you were pursuing to escape, and there was no other way to help him. This is war,. you know."

I had scarce expected so frank an admission.

"I will have to search the house for your weapon," I said. "How do I know that you will not shoot at me as I go away?"

"Do not trouble yourself," she said easily, "I will bring it to you."

She ran up the stairway and returned in a moment with a large, unloaded pistol, which she held out to me.

"I might have tried to use it again," she said with a little laugh, "but I confess I did not know how to reload it."

She handed me the pistol with a gesture

of repulsion as if she were glad to get rid of it. Her frankness changed my purpose somewhat, and I asked her how her mother fared.

"Very well, but in most dreadful alarm because of the fighting," she replied.

"It would be best for both of you, for your own safety, to remain in the house and keep the windows closed," I said.

"So I think," she replied.

I turned away, for I wished to think further what disposition to make of Kate Van Auken and her mother. It seemed that they should remain no longer at such a critical point of our line, where in an unwatched moment they might do us a great evil. Moreover, I was much inflamed against Kate because of the treacherous shot which had come so near to ending Whitestone's career. But even then I sought for some mitigating circumstance, some excuse for her. Perhaps her family had so long worked upon her that her own natural and patriotic feelings had become perverted to such an extent that she looked upon the shot .as a righteous deed. Cases like it were not new.

I thought it best to take Whitestone into my confidence.

" We can not do anything to-day," he said,
" for none of us can leave here; but it would
be well to keep a good watch upon that house
again to-night."

This advice seemed good, for like as not
Kate Van Auken, not at all daunted by her
failure, would make another attempt to escape
southward.

Therefore with much interest I waited the
coming of our second night there, which was
but a brief time away.

CHAPTER IV.

OUT OF THE HOUSE.

The night came on and I was uneasy. Many things disturbed me. The house was a sore spot in my mind, and with the dusk the signs of battle seemed to increase. Upon this dark-background the flashes from the skirmishing grew in size and intensity. From under the horizon's rim came the deep murmur of the artillery. I knew that Burgoyne was feeling his way, and more than ever it was impressed upon me that either he would break out soon or we would close in upon him and crush him. The faint pop-pop of the distant rifles was like the crackling that precedes the conflagration.

To the south there was peace, apparent peace, but I knew Burgoyne must turn his face hopefully many a time that way, for if rescue came at all it must come thence.

"Another day nearer the shutting of the

49

trap," said Whitestone, walking up and down
with his arm in a sling. I found that he could
manage his pipe as well with one hand as with
two.

The night was darker than usual, for which
I was sorry, as it was against us and in favor of
the others. Again asking Whitestone to stand
sponsor for the hollow, I approached the house.
I had repeated my precautions of the day before, placing one sentinel in front of it and another behind it. But in the darkness two men
could be passed, and I would watch with them.

From the hill top the flashes of the skirmishing seemed to multiply, and for a few moments
I forgot the house that I might watch them.
Even I, who had no part in the councils of my
generals and elders, knew how much all this
meant to us, and the intense anxiety with which
every patriot heart awaited the result. More
than ever I regretted my present duty.

The house was dark, but I felt sure in my
heart that Kate would make another attempt
to escape us. Why should she wait?

I thought it my best plan to walk in an end-
less circle around the house; it would keep sleep
away and give me the greater chance to see

anything that might happen. It was but dull and tiresome work at the best. Around and around I walked, stopping once in a while to speak to my sentinels. Time was so slow that it seemed to me the night ought to have passed, when the size of the moon showed that it was not twelve.

I expected Kate to look from the windows again and spy out the ground before making the venture; so I kept faithful watch upon them, but found no reward for such vigilance and attention. Her face did not appear; no light sparkled from the house. Perhaps after her failures her courage had sunk. Certainly the time for her venture, if venture she would make, was passing.

As I continued my perpetual circle I approached the beat of the sentinel who was stationed behind the house. I saw him sooner than I expected; he had come farther toward the side of the house than his orders permitted him to do, and I was preparing to rebuke him when I noticed of a sudden that he seemed to be without his rifle. The next moment his figure disappeared from me like the shadow of something that had never been.

Twenty yards away I saw the sentinel, upright, stiff, rifle on shoulder, no thought but of
his duty. I knew the first figure was that of
Kate Van Auken, and not of the sentinel. How
she had escaped from the house unseen I did
not know and it was no time to stop for inquiry.
I stepped among the trees, marking as closely
as I could that particular blotch of blackness
into which she had disappeared, and I had reward, for again I saw her figure, more like
shadow than substance.

I might have shouted to the sentinels and
raised hue and cry, but I had reasons—very
good, it seemed to me—for not doing so. Moreover, I needed no assistance. Surely I could
hold myself sufficient to capture one girl. She
knew the grounds well, but I also knew them.
I had played over them often enough.

The belt of woods began about fifty yards
back of the house, and was perhaps the same
number of yards in breadth. But the trees
seemed not to hinder her speed. She curved
lightly among them with the readiness of per-
fect acquaintance, and I was sure that the elation coming from what she believed to be escape was quickening her flight.

She passed through the trees and into the stretch of open ground beyond. Then for the first time she looked back and saw me. At least I believe she saw me, for she seemed to start, and her cloak fluttered as she began to run with great speed.

A hundred yards farther was a rail fence, and beyond that a stretch of corn land. With half a leap and half a climb, very remarkable in woman, who is usually not expert in such matters, she scaled this fence in a breath and was among the cornstalks. I feared that she might elude me there, but I, too, was over the fence in a trice and kept her figure in view. She had shown much more endurance than I expected, though I knew she was a strong girl. But we had come a good half mile, and few women can run at speed so far.

She led me a chase through the cornfield and then over another fence into a pasture. I noted with pleasure that I was gaining all the time. In truth, I had enjoyed so much exercise of this kind in the last day that I ought to have been in a fair way of becoming an expert.

Our course lengthened to a mile and I was within fifteen yards of her. Despite my gen-

eral disrelish for the position I felt a certain
grim joy in being the man to stop her plans,
inasmuch as she had deceived me more perhaps
than any one else.

It was evident that I could overtake her,
and I hailed her, demanding that she stop. For
reply she whirled about and fired a pistol at me,
and then, seeing that she had missed, made an
effort to run faster.

I was astounded. I confess it even after all
that had happened—but she had fired at Whitestone before; now she was firing at me. I
would stop this fierce woman, not alone for the
good of our cause, but for the revenge her disappointment would be to me. The feeling gave
me strength, and in five minutes more I could
almost reach out my hands and touch her.

"Stop!" I shouted in anger.

She whirled about again and struck at me,
full strength, with the butt of her pistol. I might
have suffered a severe, perhaps a stunning, blow,
but by instinct I threw up my right hand, and
her wrist gliding off it the pistol struck nothing, dashing with its own force from her hand.
I warded off another swift blow aimed with the
left fist, and then saw that I stood face to face

not with Kate Van Auken but with her brother Albert.

There was a look upon his face of mingled shame and determination. How could he escape shame with his sister's skirts around him and her hood upon his head?

My own feelings were somewhat mixed in character. First, there was a sensation of great relief, so quick I had not time to make analysis, and then there came over me a strong desire to laugh. I submit that the sight of a man caught in woman's dress and ashamed of it is fair cause for mirth.

It was dark, but not too dark for me to see his face redden at my look.

" You'll have to fight it out with me," he said, very stiff and haughty.

" I purpose to do it," I said, " but perhaps your clothes may be in your way."

He snatched the hood off his head and hurled it into the bushes; then with another angry pull he ripped the skirt off, and, casting it to one side stood forth in proper man's attire, though that of a citizen and not of the British soldier that he was.

He confronted me, very angry. I did not

think of much at that moment save how wonderfully his face was like his sister Kate's. I had never taken such thorough note of it before, though often the opportunity was mine.

Our pause had given him breath, and he stood awaiting my attack like one who fights with his fists in the ring. My loaded pistol was in my belt, but he did not seem to think that I would use it; nor did I think of it myself. His, unloaded, lay on the ground. I advanced upon him, and with his right fist he struck very swiftly at my face. I thrust my head to one side and the blow glanced off the hard part of it, leaving his own face unprotected. I could have dealt him a heavy return blow that would have made his face look less like his sister Kate's, but I preferred to close with him and seize him in my grasp.

Though lighter than I he was agile, and sought to trip me, or by some dexterous turn otherwise to gain advantage of me. But I was wary, knowing full well that I ought to be so, and presently I brought him down in a heap, falling upon him with such force that he lay a few moments as if stunned, though it was but the breath knocked out of him.

"Do you give up?" I asked, when he had returned to speaking condition.

"Yes," he replied. "You were always too strong for me, Dick."

Which was true, for there never was a time, even when we were little boys, when I could not throw him, though I do not say it as a boast, since there were others who could throw me.

"Do you make complete and unconditional surrender to me as the sole present representative of the American army, and promise to make no further effort to escape?" asked I, somewhat amazed at the length of my own words, and a little proud of them too.

"Yes, Dick, confound it! Get off my chest! How do you expect me to breathe?" he replied with a somewhat unreasonable show of temper.

I dismounted and he sat up, thumping his chest and drawing very long breaths as if he wished to be sure that everything was right inside. When he had finished his examination, which seemed to be satisfactory, he said:

"I'm your prisoner, Dick. What do you intend to do with me?"

"Blessed if I know," I replied.

In truth, I did not.   He was in citizens'
clothes, and he had been lurking inside our lines
for at least a day or so.   If I gave him up to
our army, as my duty bade me to do, he might
be shot, which would be unpleasant to me as
well as to him for various reasons.   If I let him
go he might ruin us.

"Suppose you think it over while I rest,"
he said.   "A man can't run a mile and then
fight a big fellow like you without getting pretty
tired."

In a few minutes I made up my mind.   It
was not a way out of the matter, but it was
the only thing I could think of for the present.

"Get up, Albert," I said.

He rose obediently.

"You came out of that house unseen," I
resumed, "and I want you to go back into it
unseen.   Do exactly as I say.   I'm thinking of
you as well as of myself."

He seemed to appreciate the consideration
and followed close behind me as I took my way
toward the house.   I had no fear that he would
attempt escape.   Albert was always a fellow of
honor, though I.could never account for the
perversion of his political opinions.

He walked back slowly. I kept as good a lookout as I could in the darkness. It was barely possible that I would meet Whitestone prowling about, and that was not what I wanted.

"Albert," I asked, "why did you shoot at Whitestone from the house? I can forgive your shooting at me, for that was in fair and open strife."

"Dick," he said so earnestly that I could not but believe him, "to tell you the truth, I feel some remorse about the shot, but the man you were pursuing was Trevannion of ours, my messmate, and such a fine fellow that I knew only one other whom I'd rather see get through with the news of our plight, and that's myself. I couldn't resist trying to help him. Suppose we say no more about it; let it pass."

"It's Whitestone's affair, not mine," I said. I was not making any plans to tell Whitestone about it.

When we came to the edge of the wood behind the house I told him to stop. Going forward, I sent the sentinel to the other side of the building, telling him to watch there with his comrade for a little, while I took his place. As soon as his figure disappeared behind the cor-

5

ner of the house Albert came forward and we hurried to the side door. We knocked lightly upon it and it was promptly opened by his sister. I could guess the anxiety and dread with which she was waiting lest she should hear sounds which would tell of an interrupted flight, and the distress with which she would see us again. Nor was I deceived. When she beheld us standing there in the dark, her lips moved as if she could scarce repress the cry that rose.

I spoke first. ·

"Take him back in the house," I said, "and keep him there until you hear from me. Hurry up, Albert!"

Albert stepped in.

"And don't forget this," I continued, for I could not wholly forgive him, "if you shoot at me or Whitestone or anybody else, I'll see you hanged as a spy, if I have to do it myself."

They quickly closed the door, and recalling the sentinel, I went in search of Whitestone.

I had some notion of confiding in Whitestone, but, after thought, I concluded I had best not, at least not fully.

I found him walking up and down in the valley.

"Whitestone," I said, "do me a favor? If anybody asks you how you got that scratch on your arm, tell him it was in the skirmish, and you don't know who fired the shot."

He considered a moment.

"I'll do it," he said, "if you'll agree to do as much for me, first chance."

I promised, and, that matter off my mind, tried to think of a plan to get Albert out of the house and back to his own army unseen by any of ours. Thinking thus, the night passed away.

CHAPTER V.

The relief came early in the morning, bringing with it the news that our army, which was stronger every day than on the yesterday, had moved still closer to Burgoyne. My blood thrilled as ever at this, but I had chosen a new course of action for myself. It would be an evil turn for me if Albert Van Auken were taken at the house and should run the risk of execution as a spy; it might be said that I was the chief cause of it.

I was very tired, and stretching myself on the turf beneath the shade of a tree in the valley, I fell into a sound sleep in two minutes. When I awoke at the usual time I found that the guard had been re-enforced, and, what was worse, instead of being first in command I was now only second. This in itself was disagreeable, but the character of the man who had supplanted me was a further annoyance. I knew

Lieutenant Belt quite well, a New Englander
much attached to our cause, but of a prying
disposition and most suspicious. The re-enforcements had been sent because of the previous attempt to break through the line at this
point, the lay of the ground being such that it
was more favorable for plans of escape than
elsewhere.

"You need not stay unless you wish," said
Belt. "No positive instructions were given on
that point. As for myself, I confess I would
rather be with the army, since much is likely to
happen there soon."

"I think things will drag for some time
yet," I said with as careless an air as I could
assume, "and I suspect that they have been
more active here than they are with the army.
Another attempt to break through our line may
be made at this point, and I believe I'd rather
remain for a day or two."

But just then, as if for the sole purpose of
belying my words about dullness at the front,
there was a sharp crackle of distant skirmishing
and the red flare of a cannon appeared on the
horizon. It called the attention of both of us
for a moment or two.

" The bullets appear to be flying over there, but if you prefer to remain here, of course you can have your wish," said Belt with sarcasm.

I did not answer, as no good excuse happened to my mind, and we went up the hillside together. I looked about carefully to see what arrangements he had made, but it was merely a doubling of the guard. Otherwise he had followed my dispositions. Belt looked at the house.

" I hear that some people are there. Who are they? " he asked.

" Only two," I replied, " women both—Madame Van Auken and her daughter."

" For us, or against us? " he asked.

" Against us," I replied. " The son and brother is in the English army with Burgoyne, over there; moreover, the daughter is betrothed to an Englishman who has just been taken prisoner by us."

I thought it best to make no disguise of these matters.

" That looks suspicious," he said, his hawk face brightening at the thought of hidden things to be found.

" They might do us harm if they could," I

said, " but they have not the power. Our lines surround the house; no one save ourselves can go to them, nor can they go to any one."

"Still, I would like to go through the house," he said, some doubt yet showing in his tone.

" I have searched it twice and found nothing," I said indifferently.

He let the matter drop for the time and busied himself with an examination of the ground; but I knew he was most likely to take ing it up again, for he could not suppress his prying nature. I would have been glad to give warning to Kate, but I could think of no way to do it.

" Who is the best man that you have here? " he asked presently.

" Whitestone—Sergeant Whitestone," I replied, glad to place the sergeant in his confidence, for it might turn out to my advantage. " There is none more vigilant, and you can depend upon all that he says."

We separated there, our work taking us in different directions. When we returned to the valley, which we had made a kind of headquarters, I heard him asking Whitestone about the Van Aukens.

"Tartars, both of 'em," said the good sergeant; "if you go in there, leftenant, they'll scold
you till they take your face off."

The look on Belt's face was proof that not
even Whitestone's warning would deter him.
At least it so seemed to me. In a half hour
I found that I had judged aright. He told me
he was not in a state of satisfaction about the
house, and since the responsibility for it lay
with him he proposed to make a search of it
in person. He requested me to go with him.

"This seems to be the main entrance," he
said, leading the way to the portico, which faced
the north, and looking about with very inquiring eyes. "Madame Van Auken and her
daughter must be much frightened by the presence of troops, for I have not yet seen the face
of either at door or window."

He knocked loudly at the door with the hilt
of his sword, and Kate appeared, very calm as
usual. I made the introductions as politely as I
was able.

"Lieutenant Belt is my senior, Miss Van
Auken," I said, "and therefore has superseded
me in command of the guard at this point."

"Then I trust that Lieutenant Belt will relax some of the rigors of the watch," she said, " and not subject us to the great discomfort of repeated searches of our house."

She turned her shoulder to me as if she would treat me with the greatest coldness. I understood her procedure, and marveled much at her presence of mind. It seemed to be successful too, for Belt smiled, and looked ironically at me, like one who rejoices in the mishap of his comrade.

She took us into the house, talking with much courtesy to Belt, and ignoring me in a manner that I did not altogether like, even with the knowledge that it was but assumption. She led us into the presence of madame, her mother, who looked much worn with care, though preserving a haughty demeanor. As usual, she complained that our visits were discourtesies, and Belt apologized in his best manner. Glad that the brunt did not now fall upon me, I deemed it best to keep silence, which I did in most complete manner.

Madame invited us to search the house as we pleased, and we took her at her word, finding nothing.. I was much relieved thereat. I had feared that Albert, knowing I would not make

another search so long as I was in command,
would not be in proper concealment.   With
my relief was mingled a certain perplexity that
his place of hiding should evade me.

Belt was a gentleman despite his curiosity,
which I believe the New England people can
not help, and for which, therefore, they are not
to be blamed, and when he had finished the vain
quest he apologized again to Madame Van
Auken and her daughter for troubling them.
He was impressed by the fine looks of the
daughter, and he made one or two gallant
speeches to her which she received very well,
as I notice women mostly do whatever may
be the circumstances. I felt some anger toward
Belt, though there seemed to be no cause for it.
When we left the house he said:

"Miss Van Auken doesn't look so dangerous, yet you say she is a red-hot Tory."

"I merely included her in a generality," I
replied. "The others of the family are strong
Tories, but Miss Van Auken, I have reason to
think, inclines to our cause."

"That is good," he said, though he gave no
reason why it should seem good to him. After
that he turned his attention to his main duty,

examining here and there and displaying the most extreme vigilance. The night found him still prowling about.

Directly after nightfall the weather turned very cool in that unaccountable way it sometimes has in the late summer or early autumn, and began to rain.

It was a most cold and discouraging rain that hunted every hole in our worn uniforms, and displayed a peculiar knack of slipping down our collars. I found myself seeking the shelter of trees, and as the cold bit into the marrow my spirits drooped until I felt like an old man. Even the distant skirmishers were depressed by the rainy night, for the shots ceased and the hills and the valleys were as silent and lonely as ever they were before the white man came.

I was thinking it was a very long and most dismal night before us, when I heard a chattering of teeth near me, and turning about saw Belt in pitiable condition. He was all drawn with the cold damp, and his face looked as shriveled as if it were seventy instead of twenty-five. Moreover, he was shaking in a chill. I had noticed before that the man did not look robust.

"This is a little hard on me, Shelby," he said, his tone asking sympathy. "I have but lately come from a sick-bed, and I fear greatly this rain will throw me into a fever."

He looked very longingly at the house.

I fear there was some malice in me then, for he had put aspersions upon my courage earlier in the day, which perhaps he had a right to do, not knowing my secret motives.

"The weather is a trifle bad, one must admit, lieutenant," I said, "but you and I will not mind it; moreover, the darkness of the night demands greater vigilance on our part."

He said nothing, merely rattled his teeth together and walked on with what I admit was a brave show for a man shaking in a bad chill. As his assistant I could go and come pretty much as I chose, and I kept him in view, bent on seeing what he would do.

He endured the chill most handsomely for quite a time, but the wet and the cold lent aggravation to it, and presently he turned to me, his teeth clicking together in most formidable fashion.

"I fear, Shelby, that I must seek shelter in the house," he said. "I would stick to the watch out here, but this confounded chill has me in its grip and will not let go. But, as you have done good work here and I would not seem selfish, you shall go in with me."

I understood his motive, which was to provide that in case he should incur censure for going into the house, I could share it and divide it with him. It was no very admirable action on Belt's part, but I minded it not; in truth I rather liked it, for since he was to be in the house, I preferred to be there too, and at the same time, and not for matters concerning my health. I decided quickly that I must seem his friend and give him sympathy; in truth I was not his enemy at all; I merely found him inconvenient.

We went again to the front door and knocked many times before any answer came to us. Then two heads—the one of Mistress Kate, the other of her mother—were thrust out of an upper window and the usual question was propounded to us.

"Lieutenant Belt is very ill," I said, taking the word from his lips, "and needs must have shelter from the cruelty of the night. We would not trouble you were not the case extreme."

I could see that Belt was grateful for the way I had put the matter. Presently they opened the door, both appearing there for the sake of company at that hour, I suppose. Belt tried to preserve an appearance in the presence of the ladies, but he was too sick. He trembled with his chill like a sapling in a high wind, and I said:

"Lieutenant Belt's condition speaks for itself; nothing else could have induced us to intrude upon you at such an untimely hour."

I fancy I said that well, and both Madame Van Auken and her daughter showed pity for Belt; yet the elder could not wholly repress a display of feeling against us.

"We can not turn any one ill, not even an enemy, away from our door," she said, "but I fear the rebel armies have left us little for the uses of hospitality."

She said this in the stiff and rather precise way that our fathers and mothers affected, but she motioned for us to come in, and we obeyed her. I confess I was rather glad to enter the dry room, for my clothes were flapping wet about me.

"Perhaps the lieutenant would like to lie

down," said Madame Van Auken, pointing to a large and comfortable sofa in the corner of the room that we had entered.

But Belt was too proud to do that, though it was needful to him. He sat down merely and continued to shiver. Mistress Kate came presently with a large draught of hot whisky and water which smelled most savorously. She insisted that Belt drink it, and he swallowed it all, leaving none for me. Madame Van Auken placed a lighted candle upon a little table, and then both the ladies withdrew.

Belt said he felt better, but he had a most wretched appearance. I insisted that he let me feel his pulse, and I found he was bordering upon a high fever, and most likely, if precautions were not taken, would soon be out of his senses. The wet clothes were the chief trouble, and I said they must come off. Belt demurred for a while, but he consented at last when I told him persistent refusal might mean his death.

I roused up the ladies again, explaining the cause of this renewed interruption, and secured from them their sympathy and a large bedquilt. I made Belt take off his uniform, and then I spread the quilt over him as he lay on the sofa, telling him to go to sleep. He said he had no such intention; but a second hot draught of whisky which Kate brought to the door gave him the inclination, if not the intention. But he fought against it, and his will was aided by the sudden revival of sounds which betokened that the skirmishing had begun again. Through the window I heard the faint patter of rifles, but the shots were too distant, or the night too dark to disclose the flash. This sudden spurt of warlike activity told me once again that the great crisis was approaching fast, and I hoped most earnestly that events at the Van Auken house would culminate first.

Belt was still struggling against weakness and sleep, and he complained fretfully when he heard the rifle shots, bemoaning his fate to be seized by a wretched, miserable chill at such a time.

" Perhaps after all the battle may be fought without me," said he with unintended humor.

I assured him that he would be all right in the morning. His resistance to sleep, I told him, was his own injury, for it was needful to his health. He took me at my word and let his eyelids droop. I foresaw that he would be asleep very soon, but he roused up a bit presently and showed anxiety about the guard. He wanted to be sure that everything was done right, and asked me to go out and see Whitestone, whom we had left in charge when we entered the house.

I was averse in no particular and slipped quietly out into the darkness. I found Whitestone in the valley.

" All quiet," he reported. " I've just come from a round of the sentinels and there's nothing suspicious. I'm going back myself presently to watch in front of the house."

I knew Whitestone would ask no questions, so I told him the lieutenant was still very ill and I would return to him; I did not know how long I would stay in the house, I said. Whitestone, like the good, silent fellow he was, made no reply.

I returned to the front door. I was now learning the way into the house very well. I had traveled it often enough. I stood for a moment in the little portico, which was as clean and white as if washed by the sea. The rain had nearly ceased to fall, and the blaze of the distant skirmishing suddenly flared up on the

6

dark horizon like a forest fire. I wondered not that the two women in the house should be moved by all this; I wondered rather at their courage. In the yard stood Whitestone, his figure rising up as stiff and straight as a post.

CHAPTER VI.

I found Belt fast asleep. The two draughts of whisky, heavy and hot, had been a blanket to his senses, and he had gone off for a while to another world to think and to struggle still, for he muttered and squirmed in his restless slumber. His hand when I touched it was yet hot with fever. He might, most likely would, be better when he awoke in the morning, but he would be flat aback the remainder of the night. He could conduct no further search in that house before the next day.

I was uncertain what to do, whether to remain there with Belt or go out and help Whitestone with the watch. Duty to our cause said the latter, but in truth other voices are sometimes as loud as that of duty. I listened to one of the other.

I drew a chair near to Belt's couch and sat

77

down. He was still muttering in his hot, sweaty sleep like one with anger at things, and now and then threw out his long thin legs and arms. He looked like a man tied down trying to escape.

The candle still burned on the table, but its light was feeble at best. Shadows filled the corners of the room. I like sick-bed watches but little, and least of all such as that. They make me feel as if I had lost my place in a healthy world. To such purpose was I thinking when Belt sat up with a suddenness that made me start, and cried in a voice cracked with fever:

" Shelby, are you there? "

" Yes, I'm here," I replied with a cheeriness that I did not feel. " Lie down and go to sleep, lieutenant, or you'll be a week getting well."

" I can't go to sleep, and I haven't been to sleep," he said, raising his voice, which had a whistling note of illness in it.

His eyes sparkled, and I could see that the machinery of his head was working badly. I took him by the shoulders with intent to force him down upon the couch; but he threw me off with sudden energy that took me by surprise.

"Let me go," he said, "till I say what I want to sáy."

"Well, what is it?" I asked, thinking to pacify him.

"Shelby," said he, belief showing all over his face, "I've seen a ghost!"

A strong desire to laugh was upon me, but I did not let it best me, for I had respect for Belt, who was my superior officer. I don't believe in ghosts; they never come to see me.

"You're sick, and you've been dreaming, lieutenant," I said. "Go to sleep."

"I'll try to go to sleep," he replied, "but what I say is truth, and I've seen a ghost."

"What did it look like?" I asked, remembering that it is best to fall in with the humor of mad people.

"Like a woman," he replied, "and that's all I can say on that point, for this cursed fever has drawn a veil over my eyes. I had shut them, trying to go to sleep, but something kept pulling my eyelids apart, and open they came again; there was the ghost, the ghost of a woman; it had come through the wall, I suppose. It

floated all around the room as if it were looking for something, but not making a breath of
a noise, like a white cloud sailing through the
air. I tell you, Shelby, I was in fear, for I had
never believed in such things, and I had laughed
at them."

"What became of the ghost?" I asked.

"It went away just like it came, through
the wall, I guess," said Belt. "All I know is
that I saw it, and then I didn't. And I want
you to stay with me, Shelby; don't leave me!"

This time I laughed, and on purpose. I
wanted to chirk Belt up a bit, and I thought
I could do it by ridiculing such a fever dream.
But I could not shake the conviction in him.
Instead, his temper took heat at my lack of
faith. Then I affected to believe, which soothed
him, and exhaustion falling upon him I saw
that either he would slumber again or weakness
would steal his senses. I thought to ease his
mind, and told him everything outside was
going well; that Whitestone was the best sentinel in the world, and not even a lizard could
creep past him though the night might be
black as coal. Whereat he smiled, and presently turning over on his side began to mutter,

by which I knew that a hot sleep was again laying hold of him.

After the rain it had turned very warm again, and I opened the window for unbreathed air. Belt's request that I stay with him, given in a sort of delirium though it was, made good excuse for my remaining. If ever he said anything about it I could allege his own words.

The candle burned down more on one side than on the other and its blaze leaned over like a man sick. It served but to distort.

I looked at Belt and wondered why the mind too should grow weak, as it most often does when disease lays hold of the body. In his healthy senses, Belt—who, like most New Englanders, believed only what he saw—would have jeered at the claims of a ghost. There was little credulity in that lank, bony frame.

But I stopped short in such thoughts, for I noticed that which made my blood quicken in surprise. Belt's uniform was gone. I rose and looked behind the couch, thinking the lieutenant in his uneasy squirmings might have knocked it over there. But he had not done so; nor was it elsewhere in the room. It had gone clean away—perhaps through the wall, like

Belt's ghost. I wondered what Whitestone's emotions would be if a somewhat soiled and worn Continental uniform, with no flesh and bones in it, should come walking down his beat.

I understood that it was a time for me to think my best, and I set about it. I leaned back in my chair and stared at the wall in the manner of those who do strenuous thinking. I shifted my gaze but once, and then to put it upon Belt, who I concluded would not come back to earth for a long time.

At the end of ten minutes I rose from my chair and went out into the hall, leaving the candle still burning on the table. Perhaps I, too, might find a ghost. I did not mean to lose the opportunity which might never seek me again.

The hall ran the full width of the house and was broad. There was a window at the end, but the light was so faint I could scarce see, and in the corners and near the walls so much dusk was gathered that the eye was of no use there. Yet, by much stealing about and reaching here and there with my hands, I convinced myself that no ghost lurked in that hall. But there was a stairway leading into an upper hall, and, as silent as a ghost myself, for which I take pride, I stole up the steps.

Just before I reached the top step I heard a faint shuffling noise like that which a heavy and awkward ghost with poor use of himself would most likely make. Nay, I have heard that ghosts never make noise, but I see no reason why they shouldn't, at least a little.

I crouched down in the shadow of the top step and the banisters. The faint shuffling noise came nearer, and Belt's lost uniform, upright and in its proper shape, drifted past me and down the steps. I followed lightly. I was not afraid. I have never heard, at least not with the proper authenticity, that ghosts strike one, or do other deeds of violence; so I followed, secure in my courage. The brass buttons on the uniform gleamed a little, and I kept them in clear view. Down the steps went the figure, and then it sped along the hall, with me after it. It reached the front door, opened it half a foot and stood there. That was my opportunity to hold discussion with a ghost, and I did not neglect it. Forward I slipped and tapped with my fingers an arm of the uniform, which inclosed not empty air but flesh and blood. Startled, the figure faced about and saw my features, for a little light came in at the door.

" I offer congratulations on your speedy recovery from fever, Lieutenant Belt," I said, in a subdued tone.

" It was quick, it is true," he replied, " but I need something more."

" What is that? " I asked.

" Fresh air," he replied. " I think I will go outside."

" I will go with you," I said. " Fevers are uncertain, and one can not tell what may happen."

He hesitated as if he would make demur, but I said:

" It is necessary to both of us."

He hesitated no longer, but opened the door wider and stepped out into the portico. I looked with much anxiety to see what sort of watch was kept, and no doubt my companion did the same. It was good. Three sentinels were in sight. Directly in front of us, and about thirty feet away, was Whitestone. The skirmishers and their rifles had not yet gone to sleep, for twice while we stood on the portico we saw the flash of powder on the distant hills.

" Lieutenant, I think we had best walk in the direction of the firing and make a little investigation," I said.

" The idea is good," he replied. " We will do it."

We walked down the steps and into the yard. I was slightly in advance, leading the way. We passed within a dozen feet of Whitestone, who saluted.

" Sergeant," said I, " Lieutenant Belt, who feels much better, and I, wish to inquire further into the skirmishing. There may be some significance for us in it. We will return presently."

Whitestone saluted again and said nothing. Once more I wish to commend Whitestone as a jewel. He did not turn to look at us when we passed him, but stalked up and down as if he were a wooden figure moving on hinges.

We walked northward, neither speaking. Some three or four hundred yards from the house both of us stopped. Then I put my hand upon his arm again.

"Albert," I said, "your fortune is far better
than you deserve, or ever will deserve."

" I don't know about that," he replied.

" I do," I said. " Now, beyond those hills
are the camp-fires of Burgoyne. You came thus
far easily enough in your effort to get out,
though Martyn, who came with you, failed, and
you can go back the same way; but, before you
start, take off Belt's uniform. I won't have
you masquerading as an American officer."

Without a word he took off the Continental
uniform and stood in the citizen's suit in which
I had first seen him, Belt being a larger man
than he. I rolled them up in a bundle and put
the bundle under my arm.

" Shake hands," he said. " You've done
me a good turn."

" Several of them," I said, as I shook his
hand, "which is several more than you have
done for me."

" I don't bear you any grudge on that account," he said with a faint laugh, as he strode
off in the darkness toward Burgoyne's army.

Which, I take it, was handsome of him.

I watched him as long as I could. You may
not be able sometimes to look in the darkness

and find a figure, but when that figure departs from your side and you never take your eyes off it, you can follow it for a long way through the night. Thus I could watch Albert a hundred yards or more, and I saw that he veered in no wise from the course I had assigned to him, and kept his face turned to the army of Burgoyne. But I had not doubted that he would keep his word and would not seek to escape southward; nor did I doubt that he would reach his comrades in safety.

I turned away, very glad that he was gone. Friends cause much trouble sometimes, but girls' brothers cause more.

I took my thoughts away from him and turned them to the business of going back into the house with the wad of uniform under my arm, which was very simple if things turned out all right. I believed that Whitestone would be on guard at the same place, which was what I wanted. I knew Whitestone would be the most vigilant of all the sentinels, but I was accustomed to him. One prefers to do business with a man one knows.

I sauntered back slowly, now and then turning about on my heels as if I would spy out the

landscape, which in truth was pretty well hid
by the thickness of the night.

As I approached the yard my heart gave a
thump like a hammer on the anvil; but there
was Whitestone on the same beat, and my heart
thumped again, but with more consideration
than before.

I entered the yard, and Whitestone saluted
with dignity.

"Sergeant," said I, "Lieutenant Belt is
looking about on the other side of the house.
He fears that his fever is coming on him again,
and he will re-enter the house, but by the back
door. I am to meet him there."

Sergeant Whitestone saluted again. I said
naught of the bundle in the crook of my arm,
which he could plainly see.

"Sergeant," said I, "what do you think of
a man who tells all he knows?"

"Very little, sir," he replied.

"So do I," I said; "but be that as it may,
you know that you and I are devoted to the
patriot cause."

"Aye, truly, sir!" he said.

We saluted each other again with great respect, and I passed into the house.

Belt was still asleep upon the sofa and his fever was going down, though he talked now and then of the things that were on his brain when awake. The candle was dying, the tallow sputtering as the blaze reached the last of it, and without another the thickness of the night would be upon us.

I ascended the stairway into the upper hall again, but this time with no attempt to rival a ghost in smoothness of motion. Instead, I stumbled about like a man in whose head hot punch has set everything to dancing. Presently Mistress Kate, bearing a candle in her hand and dressed as if for the day—at which I was not surprised—appeared from the side door.

I begged her for another candle, if the supply in the house were not exhausted, and stepping back she returned in a moment with what I desired; then in a tone of much sympathy she inquired as to the state of Lieutenant Belt's health. I said he was sleeping peacefully, and suggested that she come and look at him, as she might have sufficient knowledge of medicine to assist me in the case. To which she consented, though ever one of the most modest of maidens.

I held the candle near Belt's face, but in such position that the light would not shine into his eyes and awaken him.

" But the lieutenant would rather be on his feet again and in these garments," I said, turning the light upon Belt's uniform, which I had carefully spread out again on the foot of the couch. Then I added:

" The wearer of that uniform has had many adventures, doubtless, but he has not come to any harm yet."

I might have talked further, but I knew that naught more was needed for Kate Van Auken.

Moreover, no words could ever be cited against me.

CHAPTER VII.

IN BURGOYNE'S CAMP.

Belt awoke the next morning in fairly good health, but very sour of temper. Like some other people whom I know, he seemed to hold everybody he met personally responsible for his own misfortunes, which I take it is most disagreeable for all concerned. He spoke to me in most churlish manner, though I am fair to say I replied in similar fashion, which for some reason seemed to cause him discontent. Then he went out and quarreled with Whitestone and the others, who had been doing their duty in complete fashion.

But a few minutes after he had gone out, Madame Van Auken, who was a lady in the highest degree, though a Tory one, came to me and said she and her daughter had prepared breakfast; scanty, it is true, for the rebels had passed that way too often, but it would most likely be better than army fare, and would be good for invalids; would I be so kind as to ask Lieutenant Belt to come in and share it with them, and would I do them the further kindness to present myself at the breakfast also? I would be delighted, and I said so, also hurrying forth to find Belt, to whom I gave the invitation. He accepted in tone somewhat ungracious, I thought, but improved in manner when he entered the presence of the ladies; for, after all, Belt was a gentleman, and I will admit that he had been unfortunate. As we went in to the breakfast table I said to Belt:

"You've come out of that chill and fever very well, lieutenant. You look a little weak, but all right otherwise."

"You seem to have had your own worries," he replied a bit slowly, "for something has been painting night under your eyes."

Well, it was natural; it had been an anxious time for me in truth. But I suggested it was due to long night watches.

The ladies, as they had said, had not a great deal to offer, but it was well prepared by their own hands. They had some very fine coffee, to which I am ever partial, especially in the mornings, and we made most excellent progress with the breakfast, even Belt waxing amiable. But about the middle of the breakfast he asked quite suddenly of us all:

" Do you believe in ghosts? "

I was a bit startled, I will admit, but I rejoice to think that I did not show it. Instead, I looked directly at Mistress Kate, who in truth looked very handsome and lighted-hearted that morning, and asked:

" Do you believe in ghosts? "

" Of a certainty—of a certainty," she said with emphasis.

" So do I," said I with equal emphasis.

Madame Van Auken drank her coffee.

" I don't," said Belt. " I thought I did for a while last night. I even thought I saw one while Shelby was away from me for a while."

I rallied Belt, and explained to the ladies that the fever had given him an illusion the night before. They joined me in the raillery, and trusted that the gallant lieutenant would not see double when he met his enemies. Belt took it very well, better than I had thought. But after the breakfast, when we had withdrawn again, he said to me with a sour look:

"I do not trust those ladies, Shelby."

"Well, as for that," I replied, "I told you that Madame Van Auken was a hot Tory, of which fact she seeks to make no concealment. But I don't see what harm they could do us, however much they might wish it."

"Maybe," he said; then with a sudden change:

"Why did you say this morning that you believed in ghosts, when last night you said you didn't?"

I fixed upon him the sharp stare of one amazed at such a question.

"Belt," said I, "I am a believer in ghosts. I am also a devout believer in the report that the moon is made of moldy green cheese."

He sniffed a bit, and let me alone on that point, but he returned to the attack on the ladies. I do not know what idea had found lodgment in his head; in truth it may have been due to biliousness, but he suspected them most strongly of what he called treasonable correspondence with the enemy. I asked him what course he intended to take in the matter, and he returned a vague answer; but I soon received intimation of his purpose, for in an

hour, leaving me in charge for the time, he returned to the army. He made a quick trip, and
when he came back he told me he had reported
the case at headquarters. The general, not
knowing what else to do with the ladies, had
directed that they be sent to Burgoyne's army,
where, he understood, they had relatives.

" He said to me," said Belt, " that at this
time it would be just as well for the British to
take care of their own."

Reflecting a little, I decided that the matter
had fallen out very well. If they were in Burgoyne's camp it would release us all from some
troubles and doubts.

" You had best go into the house and notify
them," said Belt, " for they are to be taken to
Burgoyne under a white flag this very afternoon."

I found Mistress Kate first and told her what
Belt had done. She did not seem to be much
surprised. In truth, she said she had expected it.

" I trust, Mistress Kate," I said, " that while
you are in Burgoyne's army you will not let
your opinions be influenced too much by your
surroundings."

" My opinions are my own," she said, " and
are not dependent upon time and place."

Then I said something about its being a pity
that Captain Chudleigh was a prisoner in our
hands at such a time and was not with his own
army, but she gave me such a sharp answer that
I was glad to shut my mouth.

Madame Van Auken said she was glad to
go, but she would revisit her house when she
came southward with Burgoyne after he had
scattered the rebels, provided the rebels
in the meantime had not burned the house
down. Which, considering many things, I felt
I could overlook. Both promised to be ready
in an hour. I went outside and found that Belt
was able to surprise me again.

" You are to take the ladies into Burgoyne's
camp," he said. " I wished to do it myself, but
I was needed for other work."

I was not at all averse to this task, though
it had never occurred to me that I would enter
the British lines, except possibly as a prisoner.

" I wish you luck," said Belt, somewhat en-
viously. " I think the trip into the British lines
is worth taking."

Right here I may say—for Belt does not

come into this narration again—that after the war I told him the whole story of these affairs, which he enjoyed most heartily, and is at this day one among my best friends.

The preliminaries about the transfer of the ladies to Burgoyne's camp were but few, though I was exposed on the way to much censure from Madame Van Auken because of my rebel proclivities. In truth, Mistress Catherine, I think, took after her deceased and lamented father rather than her mother, who I knew had made the signal of the light to Martyn, and to Albert, who was on foot near him. But I bore it very well, inasmuch as one can grow accustomed to almost anything.

I found that during my few days' absence our army had pushed up much closer to Burgoyne, and also that we had increased greatly in numbers. Nothing could save Burgoyne, so I heard, but the arrival of Clinton from New York with heavy re-enforcements, and even then, at the best for Burgoyne, it would be but a problem. My heart swelled with that sudden elation one feels when a great reward looks certain after long trial.

Protected by the flag of truce we ap-

proached Burgoyne's lines. There were but
the three of us, the two ladies and I. Mistress
Kate was very silent; Madame Van Auken, for
whom I have the utmost respect, be her opinions what they may, did the talking for all
three. She was in somewhat exuberant mood,
as she expected to rejoin her son, thus having
all her immediate family together under the flag
that she loved. She had no doubt that Burgoyne would beat us. I could not make out
Mistress Kate's emotions, nor in truth whether
she had any; but just after we were hailed by
the first British sentinel she said to me with
an affectation of lightness, though she could
not keep her voice from sounding sincere:

"My brother will never forget what you
have done for him, Dick."

"He may or may not," I replied, "but I
hope your brother's sister will not."

Which may not have been a very gallant
speech, but I will leave it to every just man
if I had not endured a good deal in silence.
She did not take any exceptions to my reply,
but smiled, which I did not know whether to
consider a good or bad sign.

I showed a letter from one of our generals to

the sentinel, and we were quickly passed through the lines. We were received by Captain Jervis, a British officer of much politeness, and I explained to him that the two ladies whom I was proud to escort were the mother and sister of Albert Van Auken, who should be with Burgoyne's army. He answered at once that he knew Albert, and had seen him not an hour before. Thereat the ladies rejoiced greatly, knowing that Albert was safe so far; which perhaps, to my mind, was better luck than he deserved. But in ten minutes he was brought · to us, and embraced his mother and sister with great warmth; then shaking hands with me—

"I'm sorry to see you a prisoner, Dick, my lad," he said easily, "especially after you've been so obliging to me. But it's your bad luck."

"I'm not a prisoner," I replied with some heat, "though you and all the rest of Burgoyne's men are likely soon to be. I merely came here under a flag of truce to bring your mother and sister, and put them out of the way of cannon balls."

He laughed at my boast, and said Burgoyne would soon resume his promenade to New

York. Then he bestirred himself for the comfort of his mother and sister. He apologized for straitened quarters, but said he could place them in some very good company, including the Baroness Riedesel and Madame the wife of General Fraser, at which Madame Van Auken, who was always fond of people of quality, especially when the quality was indicated by a title, was pleased greatly. And in truth they were welcomed most hospitably by the wives of the British and Hessian officers with Burgoyne's army, who willingly shared with them the scarcity of food and lodging they had to offer. When I left them, Mistress Catherine said to me with a saucy curve of the lip, as if she would but jest:

"Take good care of yourself, Dick, and my brother's sister will try not to forget you."

"Thank you," I said, "and if it falls in my way to do a good turn for Captain Chudleigh while he is our prisoner, I will take full advantage of it."

At this she was evidently displeased, though somehow I was not.

Albert Van Auken took charge of me, and asked me into a tent to meet some of his fellow

officers and take refreshment; which invitation
I promptly accepted, for in those days an American soldier, with wisdom born of trial, never
neglected a chance to get something good to
eat or to drink.

On my way I observed the condition of Burgoyne's camp. It was in truth a stricken army
that he led—or rather did not lead, for it seemed
now to be stuck fast. The tents and the wagons
were filled with the sick and the wounded, and
many not yet entirely well clustered upon the
grass seeking such consolation as they could
find in the talk of each other. The whole in
body, rank and file, sought to preserve a gallant demeanor, though in spite of it a certain
depression was visible on almost every face.
Upon my soul I was sorry for them, enemies
though they were, and the greater their mis-
fortune the greater cause we had for joy, which,
I take it, is one of the grievous things about
war.

It was a large tent into which Albert took
me, and I met there Captain Jervis and several
other officers, two or three of whom seemed
to be of higher rank than captain, though I
did not exactly catch their names, for Albert

spoke somewhat indistinctly when making the
introductions. There seemed to be a degree of
comfort in the tent—bottles, glasses, and other
evidences of social warmth.

"We wish to be hospitable to a gallant
enemy like yourself, Mr. Shelby," said Captain
Jervis, "and are not willing that you should
return to your own army without taking refreshment with us."

I thanked him for his courtesy, and said I
was quite willing to be a live proof of their
hospitality; whereupon they filled the glasses
with a very unctuous, fine-flavored wine, and we
drank to the health of the wide world. It had
been long since good wine had passed my lips,
and when they filled the glasses a second time
I said in my heart that they were gentlemen.
At the same time I wondered to myself a bit
why officers of such high rank, as some of these
seemed to be, should pay so much honor to me,
who was but young and the rank of whom was
but small. Yet I must confess that this slight
wonder had no bad effect upon the flavor of the
wine.

Some eatables of a light and delicate nature
were handed around by an orderly, and all of us

partook, after which we drank a third glass of wine. Then the officers talked most agreeably about a variety of subjects, even including the latest gossip they had brought with them from the Court of St. James. Then we took a fourth glass of wine. I am not a heavy drinker, as heavy drinkers go, and have rather a strong head, but a humming of the distant sea began in my ears and the talk moved far away. I foresaw that Richard Shelby had drunk enough, and that it was time for me to exercise my strongest will over his somewhat rebellious head.

"I suppose that you Americans are very sanguine just now, and expect to take our entire army," said the oldest and apparently the highest of the officers—colonel or general, something or other—to me.

I noted that he was overwhelmingly polite in tone. Moreover, my will was acquiring mastery over Dick Shelby's humming head. I made an ambiguous reply, and he went further into the subject of the campaign, the other officers joining him and indulging slightly in jest at our expense, as if they would lead me on to boast. To make a clean confession in the matter, I felt some inclination to a little vaunting. He said something about our hope to crush Burgoyne, and laughed as if it were quite impossible.

"English armies are never taken," said he.

"But they have never before warred with the Americans," I said.

I recalled afterward that some of the officers applauded me for that reply, which was strange considering their sympathies. The old officer showed no offense.

"Have you heard that Sir Henry Clinton is coming to our relief with five thousand men?" he asked.

"No; have you?" I replied.

I was applauded again, and the officer laughed.

"You take me up quickly. You have a keen mind, Mr. Shelby; it's a pity you're not one of us," he said.

"That would be bad for me," I said, "as I do not wish to become a prisoner."

This was a bit impertinent and ungenerous, I will admit, but I had drunk four glasses of wine and they were nagging me. They filled up the glasses again, and most of them drank,

but I only sipped mine, meanwhile strengthen-
ing my rule over Dick Shelby's mutinous head.
The officer laughed easily at my reply and began to talk about the chances of the next battle,
which he was sure the British would win. He
said Burgoyne had six thousand men, English
and Hessians, and in quite a careless way he
asked how many we had.

By this time I had Dick Shelby's unruly
head under complete control, and his question,
lightly put as it was, revealed their whole plan.
Right then and there I felt a most painful regret that I had not given Albert Van Auken the
worst beating of his life when I had the chance.

I replied that I could not say exactly how
many men we had, but the number was somewhere between a thousand and a million, and
at any rate sufficient for the purpose. He
laughed gently as if he were willing to tolerate
me, and continued to put questions in manner
sly and most insidious. I returned answers
vague or downright false, and I could see that
the officer was becoming vexed at his want of
success. Albert himself filled up my glass and
urged me to drink again.

" You know, Dick, you don't get good wine

often," he said, "and this may be your last
chance."

Had not I been a guest I would have created, right then and there, a second opportunity
for giving Albert the worst beating of his life.
I pretended to drink, though I merely sipped
the fumes. The elderly officer changed his tactics a little.

"Do you think your generals are well in-
formed about us?" he asked.

"Oh, yes," I replied.

"How?"

"We learn from prisoners," I said, "and
then, perhaps, we ask sly questions from Englishmen who come to us under flags of truce."

"What do you mean?" he asked, his face
—and I was glad to see it—reddening.

"I mean," said I, "that you have brought
me into this tent with purpose to intoxicate
me and get valuable information from me. It
was a plot unworthy of gentlemen."

He rose to his feet, his eyes flashing with
much anger. But the wine I had drunk made
me very belligerent. I was ready to fight a
thousand—come one, come all. Moreover, I
leave it to all if I did not have just cause for

wrath. I turned from the officer to Albert, against whom my indignation burned most.

" I have just saved you from death, perhaps a most degrading death," I said, " and I am loath to remind you of it, but I must, in order to tell your fellow officers I am sorry I did it."

I never saw a man turn redder, and he trembled all over. It was the scarlet of shame, too, and not of righteous anger.

" Dick," he said, " I beg your pardon. I let my zeal for our cause go too far. I—I——"

I think he would have broken down, but just then the elderly officer interfered.

" Be silent, Lieutenant Van Auken," he said. " It is not your fault, nor that of any other present except myself. You speak truth, Mr. Shelby, when you say it was unworthy of us. So it was. I am glad it failed, and I apologize for the effort to make it a success. Mr. Shelby, I am glad to know you."

He held out his hand with such frank manliness and evident good will that I grasped it and shook it heartily. What more he might have said or done I do not know, for just then we were interrupted by the sound of a great though distant shouting.

8

CHAPTER VIII.

The shouting begat curiosity in us all, and we left the tent, the elderly officer leading. I perceived at once that the noise came from our lines, which were pushed up very close to those of the British and were within plain hearing distance. Among the trees and bushes, which were very dense at points, I could see in the brilliant sunshine the flash of rifle barrel and the gleam of uniform. The shouting was great in volume, swelling like a torrent rising to the flood.

I remained by the side of the old officer. He seemed anxious.

"What is it? What can that mean? It must be something important," he asked as much of himself as of me.

The reply was ready for him, as some English skirmishers came forward with an American

prisoner whom they had taken but a few moments before. The man was but a common
soldier, ragged, but intelligent. The officer put
to him his question about the shouting, which
had not yet subsided.

" That was a welcome," said the prisoner.

" A welcome! What do you mean by that? "

" Simply that more re-enforcements have
come from the south."

The officer grew even graver.

" More men always coming for them and
never any for us," he said, almost under his
breath.

I had it in mind to suggest that I be returned at once to my own army, but the arrival
of the troops or other cause created a sudden
recrudescence of the skirmishing. Piff-paff
chanted the rifles; zip-zip chirped the bullets.
Little blades of flame spurted up among the
bushes, and above them rose the white curls of
smoke like baby clouds. On both sides the
riflemen were at work.

The officer looked about him as if he intended to give some special orders, and then
seemed to think better of it. A bullet passed
through the tent we had just left. I felt that

my American uniform took me out of the list
of targets.

"Your sharpshooters seem to have come
closer," said the officer. "Their bullets fell
short this morning. I will admit they are good
men with the rifle—better than ours."

"These are countrymen," I said. "They
have been trained through boyhood to the use
of the rifle."

I was looking at the fringe of trees and
bushes which half hid our lines. Amid the
boughs of a tall tree whose foliage was yet un-
touched by autumn I saw what I took to be
a man's figure; but the leaves were so dense
and so green I was not sure. Moreover, the
man, if man it was, seemed to wear clothing of
the hue of the leaves. I decided I was mistaken; then I knew I had been right at first
guess, for I saw the green body within the green
curtain of leaves move out upon a bough and
raise its head a little. The sun flashed upon a
rifle barrel, and the next instant the familiar
curl of white smoke rose from its muzzle.

The officer had opened his mouth to speak
to me, but the words remained unspoken. His
face went pale as if all the blood had suddenly

gone out of him, and he flopped down like an emptied bag at my feet, shot through the heart.

I was seized with a shivering horror. He was talking to me one moment and dead the next. His fall, seen by so many, created a confusion in the British lines. Several rushed forward to seize the body and carry it away. Just as the first man reached it, he too was slain by a hidden sharpshooter, and the two bodies lay side by side.

Acting from impulse rather than thought, I lifted the officer by the shoulders and began to drag him back into the camp. Whether or not my uniform protected me I can not say, but I was hit by no bullet, though the skirmishing became so sharp and so hot that it rose almost to the dignity of a battle. The officer's body was withdrawn beyond the range of the sharpshooting and placed in a tent. Though he had sought to entrap me he had made handsome apology therefor, and I mourned him as I would a friend. Why should men filled with mutual respect be compelled to shoot each other?

Albert came to me there, and said in a very cold voice:

" Dick, this sudden outburst will compel you to remain our guest some time longer— perhaps through the night."

I turned my back upon him, and when he left I do not know, but when I looked that way again he was gone, for which I was in truth very glad. Yet I would have liked to ask him about Kate and her mother. . I wondered if they were safe from the stray bullets of the sharpshooters.

In the stir of this strife at long range I seemed to be forgotten by the British, as I had been forgotten by my own people. My Continental uniform was none of the brightest, and even those who noticed it apparently took me for a privileged prisoner. When I left the tent in which the officer's body lay I came back toward the American army, but the patter of the bullets grew so lively around me that I retreated. It is bad enough to be killed by an enemy, I imagine, but still worse to be killed by a friend.

The day was growing old and the night would soon be at hand. Our sharpshooters held such good positions that they swept most of the British camp. I do not claim to be a great

military man, but I was convinced that if the
British did not dislodge these sharpshooters
their position would become untenable. The
night, so far from serving them, would rather be
a benefit to their enemies, for the lights in the
British camp would guide the bullets of the
hidden riflemen to their targets.

The bustle in the camp increased, and I observed that details of men were sent to the
front. They took off their bright coats, which
were fine marks for the riflemen, and it was
evident that they intended to match our sharpshooters at their own business. Many of these
men were Germans, who, I have heard, have
always been accounted good marksmen in Europe.

Nobody caring about me, I took position on
a little knoll where I could see and yet be beyond
range. The sun, as if wishing to do his best
before going down, was shining with marvelous
brilliancy. The incessant pit-pat of the rifle fire,
like the crackling of hail, drew all eyes toward
the American line. It seemed to me that only
the speedy coming of the night could prevent
a great battle.

The crackling flared up suddenly into a volley, betokening the arrival of the fresh British skirmishers at the point of action. The little white curls of smoke were gathering together and forming a great cloud overhead. Presently some wounded were taken past.

There was a movement and gathering of men near me. Quite a body of soldiers, a company, it seemed, were drawn up. Then, with fixed bayonets, they advanced upon the American line. I guessed that the skirmishers were intended to attract the attention of our people, while this company hoped to clear the woods of the sharpshooters and release the British camp from their galling fire. The British advanced with gallantry. I give them credit for that always—that is, nearly always.

The firing had reached an exceeding degree of activity, but I did not see any man in the company fall. By this I concluded that their skirmishers were keeping our own busy, and I was in some apprehension lest this strong squad should fall suddenly and with much force upon our outposts. Forward they went at a most lively pace and preserving a very even rank, their bayonets shining brightly in the late sun. The

British boast much about their ability with
the bayonet. We know less about ours, because almost our only way of getting bayonets
was to take them from the British, which we
did more than once.

Two or three British officers gathered on
the knoll to watch the movement. Among
these was Captain Jervis, whom I liked well.
He spoke pleasantly to me, and said, pointing
at the company which was now very near to
the wood:

"That charge, I think, is going to be a success, Mr. Shelby, and your sharpshooters will
find it more comfortable to keep a little farther away from us."

He spoke with a certain pride, as if he would
hold our people a little more cheaply than his
own.

I made no reply, for another and better
answer from a different source was ready. There
was a very vivid blaze from the wood and the
crash of a heavy volley. The head of the column was shattered, nay, crushed, and the body
of it reeled like a man to whom has been dealt
a stunning blow. It was apparent that our
people had seen the movement and had gath-

ered in force in the wood to repel it, striking at
the proper moment.

The company rallied and advanced most
bravely a second time to the charge; but the
flash of the rifles was so steady and so fast that
the woods seemed to be spouting fire. The
British fell back quickly and then broke into
a discreet run into their own encampment.

"You will perceive," said I to Captain Jervis, "that our people have not yet retired for
the night."

He laughed a little, though on the wrong
side of his mouth. I could see that he felt
chagrin, and so I said no more on that point.

As if by concert our sharpshooters also
pushed up closer, and being so much better at
that business drove in those of Burgoyne.
The Germans, in particular, knowing but little
of forests, fared badly.

Though I was neither in it nor of it, I felt
much elation at our little triumph. In truth
the consequences, if not important of themselves, were significant of greater things. They
showed that Burgoyne's beleaguered battalions
could rest hope only on two things, the arrival
of Clinton or victory in a pitched battle. But

now Burgoyne could not even protect his own camp. It was reached in many parts by the fire of the sharpshooters drawn in a deadly ring around it. The night came, and as far as possible the lights in the camp were put out, but the firing went on, and no British sentinel was safe at his post.

CHAPTER IX.

MY GUIDE.

I remember no night in which I saw more misery. The sharpshooters never slept, and the dark seemed to profit them as much as the day. They enveloped the British camp like a swarm of unseen bees, all the more deadly because no man knew where they hovered nor whence nor when the sting would come. Men brave in the day are less brave at night, and every British officer I saw looked worn, and fearful of the future. I confess that I began to grow anxious on my own account, for in this darkness my old Continentals could not serve as a warning that I was no proper target. I have always preserved a high regard for the health and welfare of Richard Shelby, Esq., and I withdrew him farther into the camp. There I saw many wounded and more sick, and but scant means for their treatment. Moreover, the list

of both was increasing, and even as I wandered
about, the fresh-wounded were taken past me,
sometimes crying out in their pain.

There were many who took no part in the
fighting—Tories who had come to the British
camp with their wives and little children, and
the wives of the English and Hessian officers
who had come down from Canada with them,
expecting a march of glory and triumph to
New York. For these I felt most sorrow, as it
is very cruel that women and children should
have to look upon war.   More than once I
heard the lamentations of women and the
frightened weeping of little children.   Sometimes the flaring torches showed me their scared
faces.   These non-combatants, in truth, were
beyond the range of the fire, but the wounded
men were always before them.

It was but natural that amid so much tumult
and suspense I should remain forgotten. My
uniform, dingy in the brightest sun, was scarce
noticeable in the half-lit dusk, and I wandered
about the camp almost at will. The night was
not old before I noticed the bustle of great
preparations. Officers hurried about as if time
of a sudden had doubled its value. Soldiers

very anxiously examined their muskets and
bayonets; cannon were wheeled into more com-
pact batteries; more ammunition was gathered
at convenient points.   On all faces I saw ex-
pectation.

I thought at first that some night skirmish
was intended, but the bustle and the hurrying extended too much for that.   I set
about more thorough explorations, and it
was easy enough to gather that Burgoyne
intended to risk all in a pitched battle on
the morrow.   These were the preparations
for it.

Curiosity had taken away from me, for the
moment, the desire to go back to my own
people, but now it returned with double force.
It was not likely that my warning of the coming battle could be of much value, for our forces
were vigilant; but I had the natural desire of
youth to be with our own army, and not with
that of the enemy, at the coming of such a great
event.

But the chance for my return looked very
doubtful.   Both armies were too busy to pay
heed to a flag of truce even if it could be seen
in the night.

I wandered about looking for some means of escape to our own lines, and in seeking to reach the other side of the camp passed once more through the space in which the women and children lay. I saw a little one-roomed house, abandoned long since by its owners. The uncertain light from the window fought with the shadows outside.

I stepped to the window, which was open, and looked in. They had turned the place into a hospital. A doctor with sharp instruments in his hand was at work. A woman with strong white arms, bare almost to the shoulder, was helping him. She turned away presently, her help not needed just then, and saw my face at the window.

" Dick," she said in a tone low, but not too low to express surprise, " why haven't you returned to the army? "

" Because I can't, Kate," I said. " My flag of truce is forgotten, and the bullets are flying too fast through the dark for me to make a dash for it."

" There should be a way."

" Maybe, but I haven't found it."

" Albert ought to help you."

"There are many things Albert ought to do which he doesn't do," I said.

"Don't think too badly of him."

"I think I'll try to escape through the far side of the camp," I said, nodding my head in the way I meant to go.

"We owe you much, Dick, for what you have done for us," she said, "and we wish you safety on that account, and more so on your own account."

She put her hand out of the window and I squeezed it a little.

Perhaps that was Chudleigh's exclusive right.

But she did not complain, and Chudleigh knew nothing about it.

The British camp was surrounded, but on the side to which I was now coming the fire of the sharpshooters was more intermittent. It was the strongest part of the British lines, but I trusted that on such account the way for my escape would be more open there. At night, with so much confusion about, it would not be easy to guard every foot of ground. I walked very slowly until I came almost to the outskirts of the camp; then I stopped to consider.

In the part of the camp where I stood it was very dark. Some torches were burning in a half-hearted fashion forty or fifty feet away, but their own light only made the dusk around me the deeper. I was endeavoring to select the exact point at which I would seek to pass the lines, when some one touched me with light hand upon the shoulder.

I turned my head and saw Albert Van Auken, clad in the same cloak he wore the night he tried to counterfeit his sister. I was about to walk away, for I still felt much anger toward him, when he touched me again with light hand, and said in such a low voice that I could scarce hear:

"I am going to pay you back, at least in part, Dick. I will help you to escape. Come!"

Well, I was glad that he felt shame at last for the way in which he had acted. It had taken him a long time to learn that he owed me anything. But much of my wrath against him departed. It was too dark for me to see the expression of shame which I knew must be inprinted upon his face, but on his account I was not sorry that I could not see it.

He led the way, stepping very lightly, to-

9

ward a row of baggage wagons which seemed to have been drawn up as a sort of fortification. It looked like a solid line, and I wondered if he would attempt to crawl under them, but when we came nearer I saw an open space of half a yard or so between two of them. Albert slipped through this crack without a word, and I followed. On the other side he stopped for a few moments in the shadow of the wagons, and I, of course, imitated him.

I could see sentinels to the right and to the left of us, walking about as if on beats. On the hills, not so very far from us, the camp-fires of the American army were burning.

I perceived that it was a time for silence, and I waited for Albert to be leader, as perhaps knowing the ground better than I. A moment came presently when all the sentinels were somewhat distant from us. He stepped forward with most marvelous lightness, and in a few breaths we were beyond the line of the sentinels. I thought there was little further danger, and I was much rejoiced, both because of my escape and because it was Albert who had done such a great service for me.

"I trust you will forgive me, Albert, for

some of the hard words I spoke to you," I said. " Remember that I spoke in anger and without full knowledge of you."

He put his fingers upon his lips as a sign for me to be silent, and continued straight ahead toward the American army. I followed. Some shots were fired, but we were in a sort of depression, and I had full confidence they were not intended for us, but were drawn by the lights in the British camp. Yet I believed that Albert had gone far enough. He had shown me the way, and no more was needed. I did not wish him to expose himself to our bullets.

" Go back, Albert," I said. " I know the way now, and I do not wish you to become our prisoner."

He would not pause until we had gone a rod farther. Then he pointed toward our camp-fires ahead, and turned about as if he would go back.

" Albert," I said, " let us forget what I said when in anger, and part friends."

I seized his hand in my grasp, though he sought to evade me. The hand was small and warm, and then I knew that the deception Albert had practiced upon me a night or so before had enabled Albert's sister to do the same.

" Kate!" I exclaimed. " Why have you done this?"

" For you," said she, snatching her hand from mine and fleeing so swiftly toward the British camp that I could not stop her.

In truth I did not follow her, but mused for a moment on the great change a slouch hat, a long cloak, and a pair of cavalry boots can make in one's appearance on a dark night.

As I stood in the dark and she was going toward the light, I could watch her figure. I saw her pass between the wagons again and knew that she was safe. Then I addressed myself to my own task.

I stood in a depression of the ground, and on the hills, some hundreds of yards before me, our camp-fires glimmered. The firing on this side was so infrequent that it was often several minutes between shots. All the bullets, whether British or American, passed high over my head, for which I was truly glad.

I made very good progress toward our lines, until I heard ahead of me a slight noise as of some one moving about. I presumed that it was one of our sharpshooters, and was about to call gently, telling him who I was. I was right in my presumption, but not quick enough with my hail, for his rifle was fired so close to me that the blaze of the exploding powder seemed to leap at me. That the bullet in truth was aimed at me there was no doubt, for I felt its passage so near my face that it made me turn quite cold and shiver.

"Hold! I am a friend!" I shouted.

"Shoot the damned British spy! Don't let him get away!" cried the sharpshooter.

Two or three other sharpshooters, taking him at his word, fired at my figure faintly seen in the darkness. None hit me, but I was seized with a sudden and great feeling of discomfort. Seeing that it was not a time for explanations, I turned and ran back in the other direction. One more shot was fired at me as I ran, and I was truly thankful that I was a swift runner and a poor target.

In a few moments I was beyond the line of their fire, and, rejoicing over my escape from present dangers, was meditating how to escape from those of the future, when a shot was fired

from a new point of the compass, and some
one cried out:

"Shoot him, the Yankee spy! the damned
rebel! Don't let him escape!"

And in good truth those to whom he spoke
this violent command obeyed with most alarming promptness, for several muskets were dis-
charged instantly and the bullets flew about
me.

I turned back with surprising quickness and
fled toward the American camp, more shots pursuing me, but fortune again saving me from
their sting. I could hear the Englishmen repeating their cries to each other not to let the
rebel spy escape. Then I bethought me it was
time to stop, or in a moment or two I would
hear the Americans shouting to each other not
to let the infernal British spy escape. I recognized the very doubtful nature of my position.
It seemed as if both the British and American
armies, horse and foot, had quit their legitimate
business of fighting each other and had gone
to hunting me, a humble subaltern, who asked
nothing of either just then but personal safety.
Was I to dance back and forth between them
forever?

Some lightning thoughts passed through my mind, but none offered a solution of my problem. Chance was kinder. I stumbled on a stone, and flat I fell in a little gully. There I concluded to stay for the while. I pressed very close against the earth and listened to a rapid discharge of rifles and muskets. Then I perceived that I had revenge upon them both, for in their mutual chase of me the British and American skirmishers had come much closer together, and were now engaged in their proper vocation of shooting at each other instead of at me.

I, the unhappy cause of it all, lay quite still, and showered thanks upon that kindly little gully for getting in my way and receiving my falling body at such an opportune moment. The bullets were flying very fast over my head, but unless some fool shot at the earth instead of at a·man I was safe. The thought that there might be some such fool made me shiver. Had I possessed the power, I would have burrowed my way through the earth to the other side, which they say is China.

It was the battle of Blenheim, at least, that seemed to be waged at the back of my head, for my nose was pressed into the earth and my imagination lent much aid to facts. I seemed to cower there for hours, and then one side began to retreat. It was the British, the Americans, I suppose, being in stronger force and also more skillful at this kind of warfare. The diminishing fire swept back toward the British lines and then died out like a languid blaze.

I heard the tramp of feet, and a heavy man with a large foot stepped squarely upon my back.

"Hello!" said the owner. "Here's one, at least, that we've brought down!"

"English, or Hessian?" asked another.

"Can't tell," said the first. "He's lying on his face, and, besides, he's half buried in a gully. We'll let him stay here; I guess this gully will do for his grave."

"No, it won't, Whitestone!" said I, sitting up. "When the right time comes for me to be buried I want a grave deeper than this."

"Good Lord! is it you, Mr. Shelby?" exclaimed Whitestone, in surprise and genuine gladness.

"Yes, it is I," I replied, "and in pretty sound condition too, when you consider the fact that all the British and American soldiers in the province of New York have been firing point-blank at me for the last two hours."

Then I described my tribulations, and Whitestone, saying I should deem myself lucky to have fared so well, went with me to our camp.

CHAPTER X.

Dangers and troubles past have never pre-
vented me from sleeping well, and when I awoke
the next morning it was with Whitestone pulling at my shoulder.

" This is the third shake," said he.

" But the last," said I, getting up and rubbing my eyes.

I have seldom seen a finer morning. The
fresh crispness of early October ran through the
brilliant sunshine. The earth was bathed in
light. It was such a sun as I have heard rose
on the morning of the great battle of Auster-
litz, fought but recently. A light wind blew
from the west. The blood bubbled in my veins.

" It's lucky that so many of us should have
such a fine day for leaving the world," said
Whitestone.

The battle, the final struggle for which we

had been looking so long, was at hand. I had not mistaken the preparations in the British camp the night before.

I have had my share, more or less humble, in various campaigns and combats, but I have not seen any other battle begun with so much deliberation as on that morning. In truth all whom I could see appeared to be calm. A man is sometimes very brave and sometimes much afraid—I do not know why—but that day the braver part of me was master.

We were ready and waiting to see what the British would do, when Burgoyne, with his picked veterans, came out of his intrenchments and challenged us to battle, much as the knights of the old time used to invite one another to combat.

They were not so many as we—we have never made that claim; but they made a most gallant show, all armed in the noble style with which Britain equips her troops, particularly the bayonets, of which we have had but few in the best of times, and none, most often.

They sat down in close rank on the hillside, as if they were quite content with what we might do or try to do, whatever it might be.

I have heard many say it was this vaunting over us that chiefly caused the war.

The meaning of the British was evident to us all. If this picked force could hold its own against our attack, the remainder of their army would be brought up and an attempt to inflict a crushing defeat upon us would be made; if it could not hold its own, it would retreat into the intrenchments, where the whole British army would defend itself at vantage.

Farther back in the breastworks I could see the British gazing out at their chosen force and at us. I even imagined that I could see women looking over, and that perhaps Kate Van Auken was one of them. I say again, how like it was in preparation and manner to one of the old tournaments! Perhaps it was but my fancy.

There was no movement in our lines. So far as we could judge just then, we were merely looking on, as if it were no affair of ours. In the British force some one played a tune on a fife which sounded to me like "Won't you dare?"

"Why did we take so much care to hem them in and then refuse to fight them?" asked I impatiently of Whitestone.

"What time o' day is it?" asked Whitestone.

" I don't know," I replied, " but it's early."

" I never answer such questions before sundown," said Whitestone.

Content with his impolite but wise reply,
I asked no more, noticing at times the red
squares of the British, and at other times the
dazzling circle of the red sun.

Suddenly the British began to move. They
came on in most steady manner, their fine order
maintained.

"Good!" said Whitestone. "They mean
to turn our left."

We were on the left, which might be good
or bad. Be that as it may, I perceived that our
waiting was over. I do not think we felt any
apprehension. We were in strong force, and we
New Yorkers were on the left, and beside us
our brethren of New England, very strenuous
men. We did not fear the British bayonet
of which our enemies boast so much. While
we watched their advance, I said to Whitestone:

" I will not ask that question again before
sundown."

" I trust that you will be able to ask it then, and I to answer it," replied he.

Which was about as solemn as Whitestone ever became.

Looking steadily at the British, I saw a man in their front rank fall. Almost at the same time I heard the report of a rifle just in front of us, and I knew that one of our sharpshooters had opened the battle.

This shot was like a signal. The sharp crackling sound ran along the grass like fire in a forest, and more men fell in the British lines. Their own skirmishers replied, and while the smoke was yet but half risen a heavy jerky motion seized our lines and we seemed to lift ourselves up. A thrill of varying emotions passed through me. I knew that we were going to attack the British, not await their charge.

Our drummers began to beat a reply to theirs, but I paid small attention to them. The fierce pattering from the rifles of the skirmishers and the whistling of the bullets now coming about our ears were far more important sounds. But the garrulous drums beat on.

" Here goes! " said Whitestone.

The drums leaped into a faster tune, and we,

keeping pace with the redoubled rub-a-dub, charged into a cloud of smoke spangled with flaming spots. The smoke filled my eyes and I could not see, but I was borne on by my own will and the solid rush of the men beside me and behind me. Then my eyes cleared partly, and I saw a long red line in front of us. Those in the first rank were on one knee, and I remember thinking how sharp their bayonets looked. The thought was cut short by a volley and a blaze which seemed to envelop their whole line. A huge groan arose from our ranks. I missed the shoulder against my left shoulder —the man who had stood beside me was no longer there.

We paused only for a moment to fire in our turn, and our groan found an equal echo among the British. Then, officers shouting commands and men shouting curses, we rushed upon the bayonets.

I expected to be spitted through, and do not know why I was not; but in the turmoil of noise and flame and smoke I swept forward with all the rest. When we struck them I felt a mighty shock, as if I were the whole line instead of one man. Then came the joy of the

savage when their line—bayonets and all—
reeled back and shivered under the crash of
ours.

I shouted madly, and struck through the
smoke with my sword. I was conscious that I
stepped on something softer than the earth,
that it crunched beneath my feet; but I
thought little of it. Instead I rushed on,
hacking with my sword at the red blurs in the
smoke.

I do not say it as a boast, for there were
more of us than of them—though they used to
claim that they did not care for numbers—but
they could place small check upon our advance, although they had cannon as well as bayonets. Their red line, very much seamed and
scarred now, was driven back, and still farther
back, up the hill. Our men, long anxious for this
battle and sure of triumph, poured after them
like a rising torrent. The British were not
strong enough, and were swept steadily toward
their intrenchments.

" Do you hear that? " shouted some one in
my ear.

" Hear what? " I shouted in reply, turning to Whitestone.

" The cannon and the rifles across yonder,"
he said, nodding his head.

Then I noticed the angry crash of artillery
and small arms to our left, and I knew by the
sound that not we alone but the whole battle
front of both armies was engaged.

If the British, as it seemed, wanted a decisive
test of strength, they would certainly get it.

For a few moments the smoke rolled over us
in such volume that I could not see Whitestone,
who was but three feet from me, but I perceived
that we had wheeled a little, and nobody was
before us.   Then the smoke drifted aside, and
our men uttered a most tremendous shout, for
all the British who were alive or could walk had
been driven into their intrenchments, and, so
far as that, we were going to carry their intrenchments too, or try.

I think that all of us took a very long breath,
for I still had the strange feeling that our
whole line was one single living thing, and
whatever happened to it I felt.   The cannon
from the intrenchments were fired straight into
our faces, but our bloody line swept on.   I
leaped upon a ridge of newly thrown earth and
struck at a tall cap.   I heard a tremendous

10

swearing, long volleys of deep German oaths.
We were among the paid Hessians, whom we
ever hated more than the British for coming
to fight us in a quarrel that was none of theirs.

The Hessians, even with their intrenchments
and cannon, could not stand before us—nor do
I think they are as good as we. Perhaps our
hatred of these mercenaries swelled our zeal,
but their intrenchments were no barrier to us.
For a space we fought them hand to hand, knee
to knee; then they gave way. I saw their slain
commander fall. Some fled, some yielded;
others fought on, retreating.

I rushed forward and called upon a Hessian
to surrender. For answer he stabbed straight
at my throat with his bayonet. He would have
surely hit the mark, but a man beside him
knocked the bayonet away with his sword, call-
ing out at the same moment to me.

"That's part payment of my debt to you,
Dick."

He was gone in the smoke, and as I was
busy receiving the surrender of the Hessian and
his bayonet I could not follow him. I looked
around for more to do, but all the Hessians who
had not fled had yielded, and the fight was ours.

Burgoyne had not only failed in the pitched battle in the open field, but we had taken many of his cannon and a portion of his camp. His entire army, no longer able to face us in any sort of contest, lay exposed to our attack.

I wondered why we did not rush on and finish it all then, but I noticed for the first time that the twilight had come and the skies were growing dark over the field of battle. I must have spoken my thoughts aloud, for Whitestone, at my elbow, said:

" No use having more men killed, Mr. Shelby; we've nothing to do now but hold fast to what we've got, and the rest will come to us."

Whitestone sometimes spoke to me in a fatherly manner, though I was his superior. But I forgave him. I owed much to him.

The battle ceased as suddenly as it had begun. The long shadows of the night seemed to cover everything and bring peace, though the cries of the wounded reminded us of what had been done. We gathered up the hurt, relieving all we could; but later in the night the sharpshooters began again.

I was exultant over our victory and the certainty of a still greater triumph to come. I

rejoiced that Albert had not forgotten his debt
to me and had found a way of repayment, but
I felt anxiety also.   In the rush of the battle,
with the bullets flying one knew not whither,
not even the women and children lying in that
portion of the British camp yet intact were safe.

The wounded removed, I had nothing more
to do but to wait.   Only then did I remember
to be thankful that I was unhurt.   I had much
smoke grime upon my face, and I dare say I
was not fine to look at, but I thought little of
those things.   Whitestone, who also was free
from active duty, joined me, and I was glad.
He drew his long pipe from the interior of his
waistcoat, filled it with tobacco, lighted it and
became happy.

"It has been a good day's work," he said
at length.

"Yes, for us," I replied.   "What will be
the next step, Whitestone?"

"The British will retreat soon," he said.
"We will follow without pressing them too
hard.   No use to waste our men now.   In
a week the British will be ours."

Whitestone spoke with such assurance that
I was convinced.

CHAPTER XI.

But a dull murmur arose from the two camps, victor and vanquished. Both seemed to sleep for the morrow. I had done so much guard duty of late that I looked for such assignment as a matter of course, and this night was no exception. With Whitestone and some soldiers I was to guard one of the little passes between the hills. We were merely an alarm corps; we could not stop a passage, but there were enough behind us whom we could arouse for the purpose. The British might retreat farther into the interior, but the river and its banks must be closed to them.

We stood in the dark, but we could see the wavering lights of either camp. The murmur as it came to us was very low. The two armies rested as if they were sunk in a lethargy after their strenuous efforts of the day. I did not re-

gret my watch. I did not care to sleep. The
fever of the fight yet lingering in my blood. I
was not so old to battle that I could lie down
and find slumber as soon as the fighting ended.

"Mr. Shelby," said Whitestone, "is there
any rule or regulation against a pipe to-
night?"

"I know of none, Whitestone," I said.

He was satisfied, and lighted his pipe, which
increased his satisfaction. I strolled about a
little, watching the lights and meditating upon
the events of the day. The camps stood higher
than I, and they looked like huge black clouds
shot through here and there with bits of flame.
I believed Whitestone's assurance that Burgoyne would retreat on the morrow; but I
wondered what he would attempt after that.
Clinton's arrival might save him, but it seemed
to me that the possibility of such an event was
fast lessening. In this fashion I passed an hour
or two; then it occurred to me to approach
the British camp a little more closely and see
what movements there might be on the outskirts, if any. Telling Whitestone of my intent, I advanced some forty or fifty yards.
From that point, though still beyond rifle shot,

I could see figures in the British camp when they passed between me and the firelight.

There was one light larger than the others—near the center of the camp it seemed to be—and figures passed and repassed in front of it like a procession. Presently I noticed that these shapes passed in fours, and they were carrying something. It seemed a curious thing, and I watched it a little; then I understood what they were doing: they were burying the dead.

I could easily have crept nearer and fired some bullets into the British camp, but I had no such intent. That was the business of others, and even then I could hear the far-away shots of the sharpshooters.

The sights of this stricken camp interested me. The ground was favorable for concealment, and I crept nearer. Lying among some weeds I could obtain a good view. The figures before indistinct and shapeless now took form and outline. I could tell which were officers and which were soldiers.

Some men were digging in the hillside. They soon ceased, and four others lifted a body from the grass and put it in the grave. A

woman came forward and read from a little
book. My heart thrilled when I recognized
the straight figure and earnest face of Kate
Van Auken. Yet there was no need for me
to be surprised at the sight of her. It was like
her to give help on such a night.

I could not hear the words, but I knew
they were a prayer, and I bowed my head.
When she finished the prayer and they began
to throw in the earth, she walked away and
I lost sight of her; but I guessed that she
went on to other and similar duties. I
turned about to retreat, and stumbled over a
body.

A feeble voice bade me be more careful, and
not run over a gentleman who was not bother-
ing me but attending to his own business. A
British officer, very pale and weak—I could see
that even in the obscurity—sat up and looked
reproachfully at me.

"Aren't you rebels satisfied with beating
us?" he asked in a faint voice scarce above a
whisper. "Do you want to trample on us
too?"

"I beg your pardon," I said. "I did not see
you."

"If any harm was done, your apology has removed it," he replied most politely.

I looked at him with interest. His voice was not the only weak thing about him. He seemed unable to sit up, but was in a half-reclining position, with his shoulder propped against a stone. He was young.

"What's the matter?" I asked, sympathizing much.

"I'm in the most embarrassing position of my life," he replied, with a faint attempt at a laugh. "One of your confounded rebel bullets has gone through both my thighs. I don't think it has struck any bone, but I have lost so much blood that I can neither walk, nor can I cry out loud enough for my people to come and rescue me, nor for your people to come and capture me. I think the bleeding has stopped. The blood seems to have clogged itself up."

I was bound to admit that he had truly described his position as embarrassing.

"What would you do if you were in my place?" he asked.

I didn't know, and said so. Yet I had no mind to abandon him. The positions reversed,

I would have a very cruel opinion of him were he to abandon me. He could not see my face, and he must have had some idea that I was going to desert him.

"You won't leave me, will you?" he asked anxiously.

His tone appealed to me, and I assured him very warmly that I would either take him a prisoner into our camp or send him into his own. Then I sat my head to the task, for either way it was a problem. I doubted whether I could carry him to our camp, which was far off comparatively, as he looked like a heavy Briton. I certainly could carry him to his own camp, which was very near, but that would make it uncommonly embarrassing for me. I explained the difficulty to him.

"That's so," he said thoughtfully. "I don't want you to get yourself into trouble in order to get me out of it."

"What's your name?" I asked.

"Hume. Ensign William Hume," he replied.

"You're too young to die, Hume," I said, "and I promise not to leave you until you are in safety."

" I'll do the same for you," he said, " if ever I find you lying on a hillside with a bullet hole through both your thighs."

I sat down on the grass beside him, and gave him something strong out of a little flask that I carried in an inside pocket. He drank it with eagerness and gratitude and grew cheerful.

I thought a few moments, and my idea came to me, as good ideas sometimes do. As he could neither walk nor shout, it behooved me to do both for him. Telling him my plan, of which he approved most heartily, as he ought to have done, I lifted him in my arms and walked toward ·the British camp. He was a heavy load and my breath grew hard.

We were almost within reach of the fire-light, and yet we were not noticed by any of the British, who, I suppose, were absorbed in their preparations. We came to a newly cut tree, intended probably for use in the British fortifications. I put Ensign Hume upon this tree with his back supported against an up-thrust bough.

"Now, don't forget, when they come," I said. " to tell them you managed to crawl to this tree and shout for help. That will prevent any pursuit of me."

He promised, and shook hands with as strong a grip as he could, for he was yet weak. Then I stepped back a few paces behind him, and shouted:

" Help, help, comrades! Help! help!"

Figures advanced from the firelight, and I glided away without noise. From my covert in the darkness I could see them lift Hume from the tree and carry him into his own camp. Then I went farther away, feeling glad.

It was my intent to rejoin Whitestone and the soldiers, and in truth I went back part of the way, but the British camp had a great attraction for me. I was curious to see, as far as I could, what might be going on in its outskirts. I also encouraged myself with the thought that I might acquire information of value.

Thus gazing about with no certain purpose, I saw a figure coming toward me. One of our sharpshooters or spies returning from explorations, was my first thought. But this thought quickly yielded to another, in which wonderment was mingled to a marked extent. That figure was familiar. I had seen that swing, that manner, before.

My wonderment increased, and I decided to observe closely. I stepped farther aside that I might not be seen, of which, however, there was but small chance, so long as I sought conceal-ment.

The figure veered a little from me, choosing a course where the night lay thickest. I was unable to make up my mind about it. Once I had taken another figure that looked like it for Albert, and once I had taken it for Albert's sister, and each time I had been wrong. Now I had my choice, and also the results of experi-ence, and remained perplexed.

I resolved to follow. There might be mis-chief afoot. Albert was quite capable of it, if Albert's sister was not. The figure proceeded toward our post, where I had left Whitestone in command for the time being. I fell in be-hind, preserving a convenient distance be-tween us.

Ahead of us I saw a spark of fire, tiny but distinct. I knew very well that it was the light of Whitestone's pipe. I expected the figure that I was following to turn aside, but it did not. Instead, after a moment's pause, as if for examination, it went straight on toward the spark of light. I continued to follow. Whitestone was alone. The soldiers were not visible. I suppose they were farther back.

The gallant sergeant raised his rifle at sight of the approaching figure, but dropped it when he perceived that nothing hostile was intended.

" Good evening, Miss Van Auken," he said most politely. " Have you come to surrender? "

" No," replied Kate, " but to make inquiries, sergeant, if you would be so kind as to answer them."

" If it's not against my duty," replied Whitestone, with no abatement of his courtesy.

" I wanted to know if all my friends had escaped unhurt from the battle," she said. " I was going to ask about you first, sergeant, but I see that it is not necessary."

" What others? " said the sergeant.

" Well, there's Mr. Shelby," she said. " Albert said he saw him in that fearful charge, the tumult of which frightened us so much."

"Oh, Mr. Shelby's all right, ma'am," replied the sergeant. "The fact is, he's in command of this very post, and he's scouting about here somewhere now. Any others, ma'am, you wish to ask about?"

"I don't recall any just now," she said, "and I suppose I ought to go back, or you might be compelled to arrest me as a spy, or something of that kind."

The sergeant made another deep bow. Whitestone always thought he had fine manners. Kate began her return. She did not see me, for I had stepped aside. But I was very glad that I had seen her. I watched her until she re-entered the British camp.

When I rejoined Whitestone he assured me, that nothing whatever had happened in my absence, and, besides the men of our immediate command, he had not seen a soul of either army. I did not dispute his word, for I was satisfied.

All night long the bustle continued in Burgoyne's camp, and there was no doubt of its meaning. Burgoyne would retreat on the morrow, in a desperate attempt to gain time, hoping always that Clinton would come. The next

day this certainty was fulfilled.   The British
army drew off, and we followed in overwhelming
force, content, so our generals seemed, to wait
for the prize without shedding blood in another
pitched battle.

CHAPTER XII.

But it is not sufficient merely to win a battle. One must do more, especially when another hostile army is approaching and one does not know how near that army is, or how much nearer it will be.

It was such a trouble as this that afflicted our generals after the morning of the great victory. That other British army down the river bothered them. They wanted exact information about Clinton, and my colonel sent for me.

" Mr. Shelby," he said, " take the best horse you can find in the regiment, ride with all haste to Albany, and farther south, if necessary, find out all you can about Clinton, and gallop back to us with the news. It is an important and perhaps a dangerous duty, but I think you are a good man for it, and if you succeed, those

much higher in rank than I am will thank
you."

I felt flattered, but I did not allow myself
to be overwhelmed.

"Colonel," I said, "let me take Sergeant
Whitestone with me; then, if one of us should
fall, the other can complete the errand."

But I did not have the possible fall of either
of us in mind. Whitestone and I understand
each other, and he is good company. Moreover, the sergeant is a handy man to have
about in an emergency.

The colonel consented promptly.

"It is a good idea," he said. "I should have
thought of it myself."

But then colonels don't always think of
everything.

Whitestone was very willing.

"I don't think anything will happen here
before we get back," he said, looking off in the
direction of Burgoyne's army.

In a half hour, good horses under us, we
were galloping southward. We expected to
reach Albany in four hours.

For a half hour we rode along, chiefly in
silence, each occupied with his own thoughts.

Then I saw Whitestone fumbling in the inside pocket of his waistcoat, and I knew that the pipe was coming. He performed the feat of lighting it and smoking it without diminishing speed, and looked at me triumphantly. I said nothing, knowing that no reply was needed.

My thoughts—and it was no trespass upon my soldierhood—were elsewhere. I hold that I am not a sentimental fellow, but in the ride to Albany I often saw the face of Kate Van Auken —Mrs. Captain Chudleigh that was to be—a girl who was nothing to me, of course. Yet I was glad that she was not a Tory and traitor, and I hoped Chudleigh would prove to be the right sort of man.

" I'll be bound you're thinking of some girl," said Whitestone suddenly, as he took his pipe from his mouth and held the stem judicially between his thumb and forefinger.

" Why? " I asked.

" You look up at the sky, and not ahead of you; you sigh, and you're young," replied Whitestone.

But I swore that I was not thinking of any girl, and with all the more emphasis because I was. Whitestone was considerate, however, and said nothing more on the subject. Within the time set for ourselves we reached Albany.

Albany, as all the world knows, is an important town of Dutchmen. It is built on top of a hill, down a steep hillside, and then into a bottom by the river, which sometimes rises without an invitation from the Dutchmen and washes out the houses in the bottom. I have heard that many of these Dutchmen are not real Dutchmen, but have more English blood in them. It is not a matter, however, that I care to argue, as it is no business of mine what hobby horse one may choose to ride hard. All I know is that these Albany Dutchmen are wide of girth and can fight well, which is sufficient for the times.

Whitestone and I rode along looking at the queer houses with their gable ends to the street. We could see that the town was in a great flurry, as it had a good right to be, with our army and Burgoyne's above it and Clinton's below it, and nobody knowing what was about to happen.

"We must gather up the gossip of the town first," I said to Whitestone. "No doubt much of it will be false and more of it exaggerated, but it will serve as an indication and tell us how to set about our work."

" Then here's the place for us to begin gathering," said Whitestone, pointing to a low frame building through the open door of which many voices and some strong odors of liquor came. Evidently it was a drinking tavern, and I knew Whitestone was right when he said it was a good place in which to collect rumors.

We dismounted, hitched our horses to posts, and entered. As plenty of American soldiers were about the town, we had no fear that our uniforms would attract special attention. In truth we saw several uniforms like ours in the room, which was well crowded with an assemblage most mixed and noisy. Whitestone and I each ordered a glass of the Albany whisky tempered with water, and found it to be not bad after a long and weary ride. I have observed that a good toddy cuts the dust out of one's throat in excellent fashion. Feeling better we stood around with the others and listened to the talk, of which there was no lack. In truth, some of it was very strange and remarkable.

The news of our great battle had reached

the Albany people, but in a vague and contrary
fashion, and we found that we had beaten Burgoyne; that Burgoyne had beaten us; that Burgoyne was fleeing with all speed toward Canada; that he would be in Albany before night.
Those who know always feél so superior to
those who don't know that Whitestone and I
were in a state of great satisfaction.

But the conversation soon turned from Burgoyne to Clinton, and then Whitestone and I
grew eager.   Our eagerness turned to alarm,
for we heard that Clinton, with a great fleet
and a great army, was pressing toward Albany
with all haste.

Good cause for alarm was this, and, however much it might be exaggerated, we had
no doubt that the gist of it was the truth.

I made a sign to Whitestone, and we slipped
quietly out of the tavern, not wishing to draw
any notice ·to ourselves. Despite our caution,
two men followed us outside. I had observed
one of these men looking at me in the tavern,
but he had turned his eyes away when mine
met his. Outside he came up to me and said
boldly, though in a low voice:

" Have you come from the south? "

"No," I said carelessly, thinking to turn him off.

"Then you have come from the north, from the battlefield," he said in a tone of conviction.

"What makes you think so?" I asked, annoyed.

"You and your companion are covered with dust and your horses with perspiration," he replied, "and you have ridden far and hard."

I could not guess the man's purpose, but I took him and the others with him to be Tories, spies of the British, who must be numerous about Albany. I do not like to confess it, but it is true that in our province of New York the Tories were about as many as, perhaps more than, the patriots. We might denounce the men, but we had no proof at all against them. Moreover, we could not afford to get into a wrangle on such a mission as ours.

"You were at the battle," said the man shrewdly, "and you have come in all haste to Albany."

"Well, what if we were?" I said in some heat. His interference and impertinence were enough to make me angry.

"But I did not say from which army you came," he said, assuming an air of great acuteness and knowledge.

I was in doubt. Did the man take us for Tory spies—I grew angrier still at the thought —or was he merely trying to draw us on to the telling of what he knew? While I hesitated, he added:

"I know that Burgoyne held his own in a severe battle fought yesterday. That is no news to you. But if you go about the town a little, you will also know what I know, that Clinton, in overwhelming force, will soon be at Albany."

I was convinced now that the man was trying to draw from me the facts about the battle, and I believed more than ever that he and his comrades were Tory spies. I regretted that Whitestone and I had not removed the dust of travel before we entered the tavern. I regretted also that so many of our countrymen should prove faithless to us. It would have been far easier for us had we only the British and the hired Hessians to fight.

Whitestone was leaning against his horse, bridle in hand, looking at the solitary cloud that the sky contained. Apparently the sergeant was off in dreams, but I knew he was listening intently. He let his eyes fall, and when they met mine, he said, very simply and carelessly:

" I think we'd better go."

As I said, the sergeant is a very handy man to have about in an emergency. His solution was the simplest in the world—merely to ride away from the men and leave them.

We mounted our horses.

" Good day, gentlemen," we said.

" Good day," they replied.

Then we left them, and when I looked back, at our first turning, they were still standing at the door of the tavern. But I gave them little further thought, for Clinton and his advancing fleet and army must now receive the whole attention of the sergeant and myself.

It was obvious that we must leave Albany, go down the river, and get exact news about the British. It was easy enough for us to pass out of the town and continue our journey. We had been provided with the proper papers in case of trouble.

We had given our horses rest and food in Albany, and rode at a good pace for an hour. Not far away we could see the Hudson, a great

ribbon of silver or gray, as sunshine or cloud
fell upon it. I was occupied with the beauty
of the scene, when Whitestone called my attention and pointed ahead. Fifty yards away, and
in the middle of the road, stood two horsemen motionless. They seemed to be planted
there as guards, yet they wore no uniforms.

I felt some anxiety, but reflected that the
horsemen must be countrymen waiting, through
curiosity or friendship, for approaching travelers
in such troublous times. But as we rode nearer
I saw that I was mistaken.

"Our inquiring friends of the tavern," said
Whitestone.

He spoke the truth. I recognized them
readily. When we were within fifteen feet they
drew their horses across the way, blocking it.

"What does this mean, gentlemen? Why
do you stop us?" I asked.

"We are an American patrol," replied the
foremost of the two, the one who had questioned me at the tavern, "and we can not let
anybody pass here. It is against our orders."

Both wore ragged Continental coats, which
I suppose they had brought out of some recess
before they started on the circuit ahead of us.

I signed to Whitestone to keep silent, and rode up close to the leader.

"We ought to understand each other," I said, speaking in a confident and confidential tone.

"What do you mean?" he asked suspiciously.

I burst out laughing, as if I were enjoying the best joke in the world.

" I hate rebels," I said, leaning over and tapping him familiarly on the shoulder with my finger.

" I don't understand you," he said.

" I mean that you hate rebels too," I replied, " and that you are just as much of a rebel as I am."

" Hi should think so! Hi could tell by the look hof their countenances that they are hof the right sort," broke in Whitestone, dropping every h where it belonged and putting on every one where it did not belong.

It was Whitestone's first and last appearance on any occasion as an Englishman, but it was most successful.

A look of intelligence appeared on the faces of the two men.

"Of Bayle's regiment in Burgoyne's army, both of us," I said.

"I thought it, back yonder in Albany," said the leader, "but why did you fence us off so?"

"One doesn't always know his friends, first glance, especially in rebel towns," I said. "Like you, I thought so, but I couldn't take the risk and declare myself until I knew more about you."

"That's true," he acknowledged. "These rebels are so cursedly sly."

"Very, very sly," I said, "but we've fooled 'em this time."

I pointed to their Continental coats and to ours. Then we laughed all together.

"Tell me what really happened up there," said the man.

"It was a great battle," I said, "but we drove them off the field, and we can take care of ourselves. Six thousand British and German veterans care little for all the raw militia this country can raise."

"That's so," he said. We laughed again, all together.

"How is everything down there?" I asked, nodding my head toward the south.

"Clinton's coming with a strong fleet and five thousand men," he replied. "What they say in the town is all true."

"Small thanks he will get from Burgoyne," I said. "Our general will like it but little when Clinton comes to strip him of part of his glory."

"I suppose you are right," he answered, "but I did not think Burgoyne was finding his way so easy. I understood that the first battle at Saratoga stopped him."

"Don't you trouble yourself about Burgoyne," I said. "If he stopped, he stopped for ample reasons."

Which was no lie.

"But we must hasten," I continued. "Our messages to Clinton will bear no delay."

"Luck with you," they said.

"Luck with you," we replied, waving our hands in friendly salute as we rode away, still to the south.

Whether they ever found out the truth I do not know, for I never saw or heard of either again.

We continued our journey in silence for some time. Whitestone looked melancholy.

" What is the matter? " I asked.

" It was too easy," he replied. " I always pity fools."

He lighted his pipe and sought consolation.

CHAPTER XIII.

The night soon came and was very dark. We were compelled to stop for rest and for food, which we found at a farmer's house. But we were satisfied with our day's work. We had started, and with the appearance of fact too, the report that Burgoyne had beaten us in pitched battle. We knew the report would be carried far and wide, and Clinton would think haste was not needed. Let me repeat that to win a battle is not to win a campaign, and I hold no general's commission either.

In the morning we met a few countrymen in a state of much fright. "Clinton is coming!" was all that we could get from them. We thought it more than likely that Clinton was coming in truth, since all the reports said he and his ships ought to be very near now.

"The river is the place to look," said Whitestone.

169

We turned our horses that way, and in a few minutes stood upon its high banks.

"See," said Whitestone, pointing a long arm and an outstretched finger.

I saw, and I saw, moreover, that our search was ended. Far down the river was the British fleet, a line of white specks upon the silver bosom of the water. We could scarce trace hull or sail or mast, but ships they were without mistake, and British ships they must be, since we had none. It was not a pleasant sight for us, but it would have rejoiced the heart of Burgoyne had he been there to see.

We knew that Clinton must have several thousand men either on board the fleet or not far below, and we knew also that with such a strong force nothing could prevent his speedy arrival at Albany if he chose to hasten. I knew not what to do. Ought we to go back at once to our army with the news of what we had seen, or ought we to stay and find out more? On one side was time saved, and on the other better information. I put it to Whitestone, but he was as uncertain as I.

Meanwhile the fleet grew under the horizon of the river. We could trace masts and spars, and see the sails as they filled out with the wind. The little black figures on the decks were men.

A quarter of a mile or more below us we saw a rocky projection into the river. I proposed to Whitestone that we ride at least that far and decide afterward on further action.

We rode rapidly, but before we were half-way to the place we met men running—frightened men at that. Their condition of mind showed plainly on their faces. They wore militia uniforms, and we knew them to be some of our citizen soldiery, who are sometimes a very speedy lot, not being trained to the military business. We tried to stop them and find out why they were running and whence they came; but all we could get out of them was, "The British are coming, with a hundred ships and forty thousand men!" At last, half by persuasion and half by force, we induced one man to halt; he explained that he had been sent with the others to man a battery of four guns on the point. When they saw the British fleet coming, some of the raw militia had taken fright and fled, carrying the others with them.

12

"But the ships may not be here for an hour," I protested.

"So much the better," he said, "for it gives us the more time."

We released him, and he followed his flying comrades. Whitestone and I looked ruefully after them, but I suggested that we continue our ride to the point. Even with the ships abreast us in the river, it would be easy for us to ride away and escape the British. We rode as rapidly as the ground would allow, and soon reached the point and the deserted battery.

I could have sworn with vexation at the flight of our militia. It was a pretty battery, well planted, four trim eighteen pounders, plenty of powder, shot neatly piled, and a flag still flying from a tall pole. Whoever selected the place for the battery knew his business— which does not always happen in the military life. I looked again in the direction of the fleeing militia, but the back of the last man had disappeared.

"What a pity!" I said regretfully to White-stone. "At least they might have trimmed the rigging a little for those British ships down yonder."

"I don't understand one thing," said White-stone.

"What is it?" I asked.

He took his pipe from his mouth and tapped the bowl of it significantly with the index finger of his left hand.

"I can smoke that pipe, can't I?" he asked.

"I should think so!"

"So could you if you had a chance, couldn't you?"

"Certainly."

"Those men who ran away could fire a cannon; so could——"

"Do you mean it, Whitestone?" I asked, the blood flying to my head at the thought.

"Mean it? I should think I did," he replied. "I used to be in the artillery, and I can handle a cannon pretty well. So can you, I think. Here are the cannon, there's ammunition a-plenty, and over us flies the brand-new flag. What more do you want?"

He replaced his pipe in his mouth, sat down on the breech of a gun, and gave himself up to content. I looked at him in admiration. I approve of so many of Whitestone's ideas, and I liked few better than this. I was young.

" Good enough, Whitestone," I said. " I, as commander, indorse the suggestion of my chief assistant."

We took our horses out of the range of the guns on the ships and fastened them securely, as we were thinking of our future needs. Then we came back to our battery. Evidently the original defenders had desired the battery to appear very formidable, for in addition to their real guns they had planted eight Quaker guns, which, seen from the center of the river, would look very threatening, I had no doubt. The four guns, genuine and true, were charged almost to the muzzle.

" I think they have seen us," said Whitestone, pointing to the ships.

It was a strong fleet—frigates and sloops. It was plain that they had seen us and had not been expecting us, for the ships were taking in sail and hovering about in an uncertain way. Officers in gilt and gold stood on their decks watching us through glasses.

" Keep down, Whitestone," I said. " We must not give them any hint as to the size of our force."

" But I think we ought to give 'em a hint

that we're loaded for bear," said Whitestone.
" What do you say to a shot at the nearest
frigate, Mr. Shelby. I think she is within long
range."

I approved, and Whitestone fired. In the
stillness of a country morning the report was
frightfully distinct, and the echo doubling upon
and repeating itself seemed to travel both up
and down the river. The shot was well aimed.
It smashed right into the frigate, and there
was confusion on her decks. I fired the second
gun, and down came some spars and rigging
on the same ship. Whitestone rubbed his hands
in glee. I shouted to him to lie close, and
obeyed my own command as promptly as he.
The frigate was about to return our salute.

She swung around and let us have a broad-
side, which did great damage to the rocks and
the shore. But Whitestone and I remained
cozy and safe. A large sloop came up closer
than the frigate and fired a volley, which sailed
peacefully over our heads and made a prodigious disturbance among the trees beyond us.

" Can you get at that third gun, Whitestone? "

" Nothing easier! "

"Then give that spiteful sloop a shot. Teach her it isn't safe for a sloop to come where a frigate can't stay."

Whitestone obeyed, and his shot was most glorious. The chunk of lead struck the sloop between wind and water and must have gone right through her, for presently she began to sheer off, the signs of distress visible all over her, as if she were taking in water at the rate of a thousand gallons a minute. I clapped Whitestone on the back and shouted "Hurrah!"

But our lucky shot had stirred up the full wrath of the fleet. The ships formed in line of battle and opened their batteries on us, firing sometimes one after the other, and sometimes nearly all together. I dare say the cliffs of the Hudson, in all their long existence, have never received such another furious bombardment. Oh, it was a bad day for the trees and the bushes and the rocks, which were beaten and battered and cut and crushed by eighteen-pound shot and twelve-pound shot and six-pound shot, and the Lord knows what, until the river itself fell into a rage and began to lash its waters into a turmoil!

But Whitestone and I, with all this infernal

uproar around us, lay in our brave earthworks as snug and cozy as chipmunks, and laughed to think that we were the cause of it all. I rolled over to Whitestone and shouted in his ear:

" As soon as the eruption diminishes a little we will try a fourth shot at them! "

He grinned, and both of us embraced the earth for some minutes longer. Then the fire of the enemy began to abate. We took the first chance to peep out at them, but the volume of smoke over the river was so great and so dense that we could see the ships but indistinctly.

As for ourselves, we had suffered little. One of our guns was dismounted, but it was a Quaker, and no harm was done. The fire dying, the clouds of smoke began to float away and the ships were disclosed. Whitestone and I, peeping over our earthworks, beheld a scene of great animation and excitement. The British were working hard; there was no doubt of it. The bustle on the decks was tremendous. Officers were shouting to men and to each other; men were reloading cannon and making every preparation to renew the bombardment when their officers might order it. One frigate had come too near, and was grounded slightly in shallowing water. Her crew were making gigantic efforts to get her off before our terrible battery could blow her to pieces.

The captains were using their glasses to see what was left of us, and I could guess their chagrin when they beheld us looking as formidable and as whole as ever, barring the dismounted Quaker. Our escape from injury was not so wonderful after all. We defenders were only two, and we made a very small target; while if the battery had been crowded with men the death rate would have been prodigious.

"There goes the frigate!" I cried. " They've got her off! Give her a good-by as she goes, Whitestone! "

He was lying next to the fourth gun, and he instantly sent a shot smashing into the vessel. But the shot was like a veritable torch to a powder magazine, for the fleet attacked us again with every gun it could bring to bear. The first bombardment seemed to have aroused fresh spirit and energy for the second, and Whitestone and I, taking no chances with peeps, thrust our fingers into our ears and our heads into the ground.

But we could not keep out the heavy crash-crash of the volleys, blending now and then into a continuous roar, which the river and the horizon took up and repeated. King George must have had a pretty powder-and-shot bill to pay for that day's work.

The clouds of smoke gathered in a vast black canopy over river and ships, shore and battery. Under and through it appeared now and then the dark lines of spars and ropes, and always the blazing flash of many great guns. If the stony shores of the Hudson did not suffer most grievously, let it not be charged against the British, for they displayed a spirit and energy, if not a marksmanship, worthy of their reputation.

I rejoiced at the vigor of their fire. Its volume was so great, and they must be working so hard, that they could not know the battery was making no answer.

By and by the cannoneers waxed weary of loading and firing, and the officers of giving orders. The crash of the great guns became more infrequent. The flash of the powder bore less resemblance to continuous lightning. The smoke began to drift away. Then the defenders of the battery rose up in their courage and strength, reloaded their guns, and opened fire on the fleet.

I love to think that the British were surprised most unpleasantly. Their fire was waning, but ours was not, it seemed to them. The mischievous little battery was still there, and they had neither reduced it nor passed it. It was mirth to us to think how easily they could pass us, and yet preferred to reduce us.

"By all that's glorious," exclaimed Whitestone, "they're retreating!"

It was so. The ships were hauling off, whether to refit for another attack or to consult for future action we did not know. We gave them a few shots as they drew away, and presently they anchored out of range. Boats were launched, and men in gold-laced caps and coats were rowed to the largest frigate.

"The admiral has called a conference, I guess," I said to Whitestone.

He nodded, and we inspected our battery to see how it had stood the second bombardment. Two more Quaker guns were dismounted, but

one of them we were able to put again into fairly presentable condition. That done, we took
some refreshment from our knapsacks, and
awaited in calmness the next movement of our
enemies. As it was, we flattered ourselves that
we had made a gallant fight.

We waited a half hour, and then a boat
put out from the big frigate. Besides the
oarsmen, it contained a richly dressed officer and a white flag. They came directly toward us.

"A flag of truce and a conference," I said.
" Shall we condescend, Whitestone? "

" Oh, yes," replied Whitestone. " We
ought to hear what they have to say."

" Then you remain in command of the battery," I said, " and I will meet the officer."

I scrambled down the high cliff to the
water's edge and awaited the boat, which I
was determined should not come too near.
When it came within speaking distance, I hailed
the officer and ordered him to stop.

" I am Captain Middleton," he called, " and
I am commissioned by our commander to speak
to your commander."

" General Arnold saw you coming," I said,

"and sent me to meet you and hear what you have to say."

"General Arnold!" he exclaimed in surprise.

"Yes, General Arnold, the commander of our battery," I replied.

I mentioned General Arnold because of his great reputation then as a fighting general. And a fighting general he was, too; I will say it, traitor though he afterward proved to be.

"I thought General Arnold was with Gates," said the officer.

"Oh, they quarreled," I replied airily, which was the truth, "and General Arnold, being relieved of his command up there, has come down here to fight this battery. You have seen for yourself that he knows how to do it."

"It is true," he said, "your fire was very warm."

He looked up at the battery, but I would not let him come within fifty feet of the shore, and he could see nothing save the earthworks and some of the gun muzzles.

"It can be made warmer," I said confidently, not boastingly.

"I have come to summon you to surrender," he said. "We will offer you good terms."

"Surrender!" I laughed in scorn. "Why, my dear captain, you have made no impression upon us yet, while we have scarred your ships a bit."

"That is a fact," he said. "You have handled your eighteen-pounders well."

"Twenty-four pounders," I corrected.

"I did not know they were so heavy," he said. "That accounts for the strength of your fire."

He seemed pleased at the discovery. It made an excuse for his side.

"No doubt General Arnold can do something with a battery of twelve twenty-four pounders," he began.

"Eighteen twenty-four pounders," I corrected. "You can not see all the muzzles."

He looked very thoughtful. I knew that he was impressed by the exceeding strength of our battery.

"But about the proposition to surrender," he began.

"I will not take such an offer to General Arnold," I exclaimed indignantly. "In fact, I have my instructions from him. He'll sink every ship you have, or be blown to pieces himself."

Captain Middleton, after this emphatic declaration, which I am sure I made in a most convincing manner, seemed to think further talk would be a waste, and gave the word to his oarsmen to pull back to his ship.

" Good day," he said very courteously.

" Good day," said I with equal courtesy. Then I climbed back up the cliff and re-enforced the garrison. I watched Middleton as he approached the flagship. He mounted to the deck and the officers crowded around him. In a half hour the ships bore up again, formed line of battle, and opened upon us a third terrific bombardment, which we endured with the same calmness and success. When they grew tired we gave them a few shots, which did some execution, and then, to our infinite delight, they slipped their cables and fell back down the river.

" When they find out what we really are they'll come again to-morrow and blow us to splinters," said Whitestone.

" Yes, but we'll be far away from here then," said I, " and we may have held them back a day at least. Why, man, even an hour is worth much to our army up yonder!"

We were in a state of supreme satisfaction, also in a state of hurry. There was nothing more for us to do in the south, and it was our business to hasten northward with the news we had. I rejoiced greatly. I hoped that Clinton would continue to fiddle his time away below Albany, impressed by the risks he was taking, thanks to our brave battery.

We found our horses nearly dead from fright, but a few kicks restored life, and we rode northward in all haste. At Albany we changed horses, evaded questions, and resumed our ride. In the night we reached our own camp, and as soon as we had reported sought the rest we needed so badly, and, I think, deserved so well.

CHAPTER XIV.

THE PURSUIT OF CHUDLEIGH.

Having returned, I expected to share in the pursuit of Burgoyne, and wondered to what particular duty I would be assigned. But a man never knows at seven o'clock what he will be doing at eight o'clock, and before eight o'clock had come I was called by the colonel of our regiment.

"Mr. Shelby," he said, "you have already shown yourself intelligent and vigilant on important service."

I listened, feeling sure that I was going to have something very disagreeable to do. You can depend upon it when your superior begins with formal flattery. I had just finished one important task, but the more you do the more people expect of you.

"One of our prisoners has escaped," he said; "a keen-witted man who knows the country.

He has escaped to the south. As you know so well, Sir Henry Clinton is, or has been, advancing up the Hudson with a strong force to the aid of Burgoyne, whom nothing else can save from us. This man—this prisoner who has escaped—must not be permitted to reach Clinton with the news that Burgoyne is almost done for. It was important before the last battle that no messenger from Burgoyne should pass through our lines; it is still more important to-day. You understand?"

I bowed, as a sign that I understood.

"This escaped prisoner knows everything that has happened," he resumed, "and he must be overtaken. He will probably follow the direct road along the river, as he knows that haste is necessary. How many men do you want?"

I named Whitestone and a private, a strong, ready-witted fellow named Adams.

"What is the name of the man we are to capture?" I asked.

"Chudleigh—Captain Ralph Chudleigh," he replied. "A tall man, dark hair and eyes, twenty-six to twenty-eight years of age. Do you know him?"

13

I replied that I knew him.

"So much the better," said our colonel with much delight. "Aside from your other qualifications, Mr. Shelby, you are the man of all men for this duty. Chudleigh will undoubtedly attempt to disguise himself, but since you know him so well he can scarce hide his face from you. But remember that he must be taken, dead or alive."

I had not much relish for the mission in the first place, and, for reasons, less relish when I knew that Chudleigh was the man whom I was to take. But in such affairs as these it is permitted to the soldier to choose only the one thing, and that is, to obey.

We set out at once over the same road we had traveled twice so recently. Three good horses had been furnished us, and we were well armed. For a while we rode southward with much speed, and soon left behind us the last detachment of our beleaguering army.

One question perplexed me: Would Chudleigh be in his own British uniform, which he wore when he escaped, or did he manage to take away with him some rags of Continental attire, in which he would clothe himself first chance?

I could answer it only by watching for all men of suspicious appearance, no matter the cut or color of their clothing.

We galloped along a fair road, but we met no one. Quiet travelers shun ground trodden by armies. It was past the noon hour when we came to a small house not far from the roadside. We found the farmer who owned it at home, and in answer to our questions, fairly spoken, he said three men had passed that day, two going north and one going south, all dressed as ordinary citizens. I was particularly interested in the one going south, and asked more about him.

" He was tall, dark, and young," said the farmer. " He looked like a man of small consequence, for his clothing was ragged and his face not overclean. He wanted food, and he ate with much appetite."

I asked if the man had paid for his dinner, and the farmer showed me silver fresh from the British mint. I could well believe that this was Chudleigh. However wary and circumspect he might be he was bound to have food, and he could find it only by going to the houses he saw on his southern journey.

I was confirmed in my belief an hour later,
when we met a countryman on foot, who at
first evinced a great desire to run away from
us, but who stopped, seeing our uniforms. He
explained that he knew not whom to trust, for
a short while before he was riding like ourselves;
now he had no horse; a ragged man meeting
him in the road had presented a pistol at his
head and ordered him to give up his horse,
which he did with much promptness, as the
man's finger lay very caressingly upon the trigger of the pistol.

" That was Chudleigh without doubt," I said
to Whitestone, " and since he also is now
mounted we must have a race for it."

He agreed with me, and we whipped our
horses into a gallop again. In reality I had
not much acquaintance with Chudleigh, but I
trusted that I would know his face anywhere.
Secure in this belief we pressed on.

"Unless he's left the road to hide—and that's
not probable, for he can't afford delay—we
ought to overhaul him soon," said Whitestone.

The road led up and down a series of lightly
undulating hills. Just when we reached one
crest we saw the back of a horseman on the

next crest, about a quarter of a mile ahead of us. By a species of intuition I knew that it was Chudleigh. Aside from my intuition, all the probabilities indicated Chudleigh, for we had the word of the dismounted farmer that his lead of us was but short.

"That's our man!" exclaimed Whitestone, echoing our thought.

As if by the same impulse, all three of us clapped spur to horse, and forward we went at a gallop that sent the wind rushing past us. We were much too far away for the fugitive to hear the hoof-beats of our horses, but by chance, I suppose, he happened to look back and saw us coming at a pace that indicated zeal. I saw him give his mount a great kick in the side, and the horse bounded forward so promptly that in thirty seconds the curve of the hill hid both horse and rider from our view. But that was not a matter discouraging to us. The river was on one side of us not far away, and on the other cultivated fields inclosed with fences. Chudleigh could not leave the road unless he dismounted. He was bound to do one of two things, outgallop us or yield.

We descended our hill and soon rose upon

the slope of Chudleigh's.   When we reached
the crest, we saw him in the hollow beyond
urging his horse to its best speed.   He was
bent far over upon the animal's neck, and oc- ,
casionally he gave him lusty kicks in the
side.   It was evident to us that whatever
speed might be in that horse Chudleigh would
get it out of him.   And so would I, thought
I, if I were in his place.   A fugitive could
scarce have more inducement than Chudleigh
to escape.

Measuring the distance with my eye, I concluded that we had gained a little.   I drew from
it the inference that we would certainly overtake him.   Moreover, Chudleigh was making
the mistake of pushing his horse too hard at
the start.

It is better to pursue than to be pursued,
and a great elation of spirits seized me.   The
cool air rushing into my face and past my ears
put bubbles in my blood.

" This beats watching houses in the night,
does it not, Whitestone? " I said.

" Aye, truly," replied the sober sergeant,
" unless he has a pistol and concludes to use
it."

"We will not fire until he does, or shows intent to do so," I said.

Whitestone and Adams nodded assent, and we eased our horses a bit that we might save their strength and speed. This maneuver enabled the fugitive to gain slightly upon us, but we felt no alarm; instead we were encouraged, for his horse was sure to become blown before ours put forth their best efforts.

Chudleigh raised up once to look back at us. Of course it was too far for us to see the expression of his face, but in my imagination anxiety was plainly writ there.

" How long a race will it be, do you think? " I asked Whitestone.

"About four miles," he said, "unless a stumble upsets our calculations, and I don't think we'll have the latter, for the road looks smooth all the way."

The fugitive began to kick his horse with more frequency, which indicated increased anxiety.

" It won't be four miles," I said to Whitestone.

"You're right," he replied; "maybe not three."

In truth it looked as if Whitestone's second thought were right. We began to gain without the necessity of urging our horses. Chudleigh already had driven his own animal to exhaustion. I doubted if the race would be a matter of two miles. I wondered why he did not try a shot at us with his pistols. Bullets are often great checks to the speed of pursuers, and Chudleigh must have known it.

At the end of a mile we were gaining so rapidly that we could have reached the fugitive with a pistol ball, but I was averse to such rude methods, doubly so since he showed no intent on his own part to resort to them.

A half mile ahead of us I saw a small house in a field by the roadside, but I took no thought of it until Chudleigh reached a parallel point in the road; then we were surprised to see him leap to the ground, leave his horse to go where it would, climb the fence, and rush toward the house. He pushed the door open, ran in, and closed it behind him.

I concluded that he had given up all hope of escape except through a desperate defense, and I made hasty disposition of my small command. I was to approach the house from one side,

Whitestone from another, and Adams from a third.

We hitched our horses and began our siege of the house, from which no sound issued. I approached from the front, using a fence as shelter. When I was within half a pistol shot the door of the house was thrown open with much force and rudeness, and a large woman, a cocked musket in her hand and anger on her face, appeared. She saw me, and began to berate me rapidly and wrathfully, at the same time making threatening movements with the musket. She cried out that she had small use for those who were Tories now and Americans then, and robbers and murderers always. I explained that we were American soldiers in pursuit of an escaped prisoner of importance who had taken refuge in her house, and commanded her to stand aside and let us pass.

For answer she berated me more than ever, saying that it was but a pretext about a prisoner, and her husband was a better American than we. That put a most uncomfortable suspicion in my mind, and, summoning Whitestone, we held parley with her.

"You have pursued my husband until there is scarce a breath left in his body," she said.

Whereupon, having pacified her to some extent, we went into the house and found that she spoke the truth. Her husband was stretched upon a bed quite out of breath, in part from his gallop and more from fright. We could scarce persuade him that we were not those outlaws who belonged to neither army but who preyed upon whomsoever they could.

Making such brief apologies as the time allowed, we mounted our horses and resumed the search.

"It was a mistake," said Whitestone.

I admitted that he spoke the truth, and resolved I would trust no more to intuitions, which are sent but to deceive us.

Anxiety now took me in a strong grip. Our mistaken chase had caused us to come very fast, and since we saw nothing of Chudleigh, I feared lest we had passed him in some manner. It therefore cheered me much, a half hour later, when I saw a stout man, whom I took to be a farmer, jogging comfortably toward us on a stout nag as comfortable-looking as himself. He was not like the other, suspicious and afraid, and I was glad of it, for I said to myself that here was a man of steady habit and intelligence, a man who would tell us the truth and tell it clearly.

He came on in most peaceable and assuring fashion, as if not a soldier were within a thousand miles of him. I hailed him, and he replied with a pleasant salutation.

" Have you met a man riding southward? " I said.

" What kind of a man? " he asked.

" A large man in citizen's dress," I replied.

" Young, or old? "

" Young—twenty-six or twenty-eight."

" Anything else special about him? "

" Dark hair and eyes and dark complexion; his horse probably very tired."

" What do you want with this man? " he asked, stroking a red whisker with a contemplative hand.

" He is an escaped prisoner," I replied, " and it is of the greatest importance that we recapture him."

"Did you say he was rather young? Looked like he might be six and twenty or eight and twenty? " he asked.

" Yes, that is he," I said eagerly.

" Tall, rather large? "

" The very man."

" Dark hair and eyes and dark complexion? "

" Exactly! Exactly! "

" His horse very tired? "

" Our man beyond a doubt! Which way did he go? "

" Gentlemen, I never saw or heard of such a man," he replied gravely, laying switch to his horse and riding on.

We resumed our journey, vexation keeping us silent for some time.

" Our second mistake," said Whitestone at length.

As I did not answer, he added:

" But the third time means luck."

" I doubt it," I replied. My disbelief in signs and omens was confirmed by the failure of my intuition.

CHAPTER XV.

We were forced to ride with some slowness owing to the blown condition of our horses, and anxiety began to gnaw me to the marrow. We had come so fast that the time to overtake Chudleigh, if in truth we had not passed him already, had arrived. In such calculations I was interrupted by the sight of a loose horse in the road, saddled and bridled, but riderless. He was in a lather, like ours, and I guessed at once that this was the horse Chudleigh had taken. In some manner—perhaps he had seen us, though unseen himself—he had learned that he was pursued hotly, and, fearing to be overtaken, had abandoned his horse and taken to the woods and fields. Such at least was my guess.

I esteemed it great good luck when I saw a man standing in the edge of a cornfield staring at us. He was a common-looking fellow with a dirty face. Stupid, I thought, but perhaps he has seen what happened here and can tell me. I hailed him, and he answered in a thick voice, though not unfriendly. I asked him about the horse, and if he knew who had abandoned him there. He answered with that degree of excitement a plowboy would most likely show on such occasions that he was just going to tell us about it. I bade him haste with his narration.

He said, with thick, excited tongue, that a man had come along the road urging his horse into a gallop. When they reached the field the horse broke down and would go no farther. The rider, after belaboring him in vain, leaped down, and, leaving the horse to care for himself, turned from the road.

This news excited Whitestone, Adams, and me. It was confirmation of our suspicions, and proof also that we were pressing Chudleigh hard.

" How long ago was that? " I asked.

" Not five minutes," replied the plowman.

" Which way did he go? " I asked, my excitement increasing.

" He took the side road yonder," replied the plowman.

"What road?" exclaimed Whitestone, breaking in.

"The road that leads off to the right—yonder, at the end of the field."

I was about to set off in a gallop, but it occurred to me as a happy thought that this fellow, knowing the country so well, would be useful as a guide. I ordered him to get on the loose horse, now somewhat rested, and lead the way. He demurred. But it was no time to be squeamish or overpolite, so I drew my pistol and warned him. Thereupon he showed himself a man of judgment and mounted, and taking the lead of us, obedient to my command, also showed himself to be a very fair horseman.

In a few seconds we entered the diverging road, which was narrow, scarce more than a path. It led between two fields, and then through some thin woods.

"You are military folks," said our guide, turning a look upon me. "Is the man you are after a deserter?"

"No," said I, "a spy."

"If you overtake him and he fights, I don't have any part in it," he said.

"You needn't risk your skin," I said. "It is enough for you to guide us."

I laughed a bit at his cowardice; but after all I had no right to laugh. It was no business of his to do our fighting for us.

"Perhaps he has turned into these woods," said Whitestone.

"No, he has gone on," said our guide, "I can see his footsteps in the dust."

Traces like those of human footsteps were in truth visible in the dust, but we had no time to stop for examination. We rode on, watching the country on either side of the road. The heat and animation of the chase seemed to affect our guide, heavy plowman though he was.

"There go his tracks still!" he cried. "See, by the edge of the road, by the grass there?"

"We'll catch him in five minutes!" cried Adams, full of enthusiasm.

Our guide was ten feet in front of me, leaning over and looking about with much eagerness. A curve in the road two or three hundred yards ahead became visible. Suddenly I noticed an increase of excitement in the expression of our guide.

"I see him! I see him!" he cried.

"Where? Where?" I shouted.

"Yonder! yonder! Don't you see, just turning the curve in the road? There! He has seen us too, and is drawing a pistol. Gentlemen, remember your agreement: I'm not to do any of the fighting. I will fall back."

"All right!" I cried. "You've done your share of the business. Drop back.—Forward, Whitestone! We've got our man now!"

In a high state of excitement we whipped our horses forward, paying no further attention to the plowman, for whom in truth we had use no longer. Our horses seemed to share our zeal, and recalled their waning strength and spirits. Forward we went at a fine pace, all three of us straining our eyes to catch the first glimpse of the fugitive when we should turn the curve around the hill.

"Two to one I beat you, Whitestone!" I said.

"Then you'll have to push your horse more," said the sergeant, whose mount was neck and neck with mine.

In truth it looked as if he would pass me, but I managed to draw a supreme effort from my horse and we went ahead a little. How-

14

ever, I retained the advantage but a few moments. Whitestone crept up again, and we continued to race neck and neck. Adams, upon whom we had not counted as a formidable antagonist, overhauled us, though he could not pass us.

Thus we three, side by side, swept around the curve, and the command to the fugitive to halt and surrender was ready upon our lips.

The turn of the curve brought us into a wide and bare plain, and we pulled up astonished. Nowhere was a human being visible, and upon that naked expanse concealment was impossible.

We stared at each other in amazement, and then in shame. The truth of the trick struck me like a rifle shot. Why did I wait until he was gone to remember something familiar in the voice of that plowman, something known in the expression of that face? I think the truth came to me first, but before I said anything Whitestone ejaculated:

" Chudleigh! "

" Without doubt," I replied.

" I told you the third time would not fail," he said.

"I wish it had failed," I exclaimed in wrath and fury, "for he has made fools of us!"

We wheeled our horses about as if they turned on pivots and raced back after the wily plowman. I swore to myself a mighty oath that I would cease to be certain about the identity of anybody, even of Whitestone himself. Whitestone swore out loud about a variety of things, and Adams was equal to his opportunities.

We were speedily back in the main road. I doubted not that Chudleigh had hurried on toward the south. In truth he could not afford to do otherwise, and he would profit as fast as he could by the breathing space obtained through the trick he had played upon us. I wondered at the man's courage and presence of mind, and it was a marvel that we had not gone much farther on the wrong road before detecting the stratagem.

The road lay across a level country and we saw nothing of Chudleigh. Nevertheless we did not spare our weary horses. We were sure he was not very far ahead, and it was no time for mercy to horseflesh. Yet I thought of the

poor brutes. I said to Whitestone I trusted
they would last.

"As long as his, perhaps," replied Whitestone.

But the truth soon became evident that he
was wrong in part. We heard a great groan,
louder than a man can make, and Adams's horse
went down in a cloud of dust. I pulled up just
enough to see that Adams was not hurt, and
to shout to him:

"Follow us as best you can!"

Then on we went. Far ahead of us in the
road we saw a black speck. Whether man,
beast, or a stump, I could not say, but we hoped
it was Chudleigh.

"See, it moves!" cried Whitestone.

Then it was not a stump, and the chance
that it was Chudleigh increased. Soon it became apparent that the black object was not
only moving, but moving almost as fast as we.
By and by we could make out the figure of a
man lashing a tired horse. That it was Chudleigh no longer admitted of doubt.

"We'll catch him yet! His trick shall not
avail him!" I cried exultingly to Whitestone.

The wise sergeant kept silent and saved his

breath. I looked back once and saw a man running after us, though far away. I knew it was Adams following us on foot, faithful to his duty.

I felt a great shudder running through the horse beneath me, and then the faithful animal began to reel like a man in liquor. I could have groaned in disappointment, for I knew these signs betokened exhaustion, and a promise that the pursuit would be left to Whitestone alone. But even as my mind formed the thought, Whitestone's horse fell as Adams's had fallen. My own, seeing his last comrade go down, stopped stock still, and refused to stir another inch under the sharpest goad.

"What shall we do?" I cried to Whitestone.

"Follow on foot!" he replied. "His horse must be almost as far gone as ours!"

We paused only to snatch our pistols from the holsters, and then on foot we pierced the trail of dust Chudleigh's horse had left behind him. The fine dust crept into eyes, nose, mouth, and ears. I coughed and spluttered, and just as I was rubbing sight back into my eyes I heard a joyful cry from Whitestone. I was able

to see then through the dust, and I beheld
Chudleigh abandoning his horse and taking to
the woods on foot.

" It's a foot race now, and not a horse race! "
I said to Whitestone.

" Yes, and we must still win! " he replied.

Poor Adams was lost to sight behind us.

About two hundred yards from the road
the woods began. I feared that if Chudleigh
reached these he might elude us, and I pushed
myself as I had pushed my horse. Being long-
legged and country bred, I am a fair runner;
in fact, it is a muscular talent upon which I
used to pride myself. The sergeant puffed
much at my elbow, but managed to keep his
place.

I now perceived with much joy that we
could outrun Chudleigh. When he dashed into
the woods we had made a very smart gain upon
him, and in truth were too near for him to
elude us by doubling or turning in the under-
growth. Despite the obstacle of the trees and
the bushes we were yet able to keep him in
view, and, better acquainted with this sort of
work than he, we gained upon him even more
rapidly than before. We flattered ourselves

that we would soon have him.   Though it was
a heavy draught upon my breath, I shouted
with all my might to Chudleigh to stop and
yield.   For answer he whirled around and fired
a pistol at us.   The sergeant grunted, and
stopped.

"Go on and take him yourself!" he said
hastily to me. "His bullet's in my leg!   No
bones broke, but I can't run any more!   Adams
will take care of me!"

Obedient to his command and my own impulse I continued the chase.   Perhaps if I had
been cooler in mind I might not have done so,
for Chudleigh had proved himself a man;   he
probably had another pistol, and another bullet
in that other pistol;   in case that other bullet
and I met, I knew which would have to yield,
but I consoled myself with the reflection that I
too had a pistol and some acquaintance with its
use.

Chudleigh did not look back again, and perhaps did not know that he was now pursued by
only one man.   He continued his flight as zeal-
ously as ever.   As I may have observed before,
and with truth too, it incites one's courage wonderfully to have a man run from him, and see-

ing Chudleigh's back I began to feel quite com-
petent to take him alone. We wound about
among the trees at a great rate. I was gaining,
though I was forced to pump my breath up
from great depths. But I was consoled by the
reflection that, however tired I might be, surely
he fared no better. I shouted to him again and
again, to stop, but he ran as if he were born deaf.

Presently I noticed that he was curving back
toward the road, and I wondered at his purpose.
A moment later he burst from the trees into
the open ground. I was within fair pistol shot,
and, with trees and bushes no longer obstruct-
ing, he was a good target. I doubted not that
I could hit him, and since he would not stop
for my voice, I must see if a bullet would make
him more obedient.

I raised my pistol and took the good aim
which one can do running if he has had the
practice. But my heart revolted at the shot.
If I could risk so much for Kate Van Auken's
brother, surely I could risk something for Kate
Van Auken's lover. I do not take praise to myself for not shooting Chudleigh, as I was thinking that if I did fire the shot I would have but
a poor tale to tell to Mistress Catherine.

I let down the hammer of the pistol and stuffed the weapon into my pocket. Chudleigh was now running straight toward the road. My wonder what his purpose might be increased.

Of a sudden he drew a second pistol and fired it at me, but his bullet sped wide of the mark. He threw the pistol on the ground and tried to run faster.

I thought that when he reached the road he would follow it to the south, hoping to shake me off; but, very much to my surprise, he crossed it, and kept a straight course toward the river. Then I divined that he being a good swimmer, hoped I was not, and that thus he might escape me. But I can swim as well as run, and I prepared my mind for the event. When he reached the river he threw off his coat with a quick movement and sprang boldly into the stream. But I was ready. I threw my own coat aside—the only one I had—and leaped into the water after him.

If I was a good swimmer, so was Chudleigh. When I rose from my first splash he was already far from me, floating partly with the stream, and following a diagonal course toward the farther shore. I swam after him with vigorous strokes. Curiously enough, the severe exertion to which I had been subjecting myself on land did not seem to affect me in the water. I suppose a new set of muscles came into play, for I felt fresh and strong. Moreover, I resolved that I would cling to Chudleigh to the very last; that I would not let him by any chance escape me. I felt again that the entire fate of the great campaign depended upon me, and me alone. With such a feeling, one's sense of importance grows much, and I think it made my arm stronger also, which was what I needed more particularly just then.

Chudleigh dived once and remained under water a long time, with the probable intent of deceiving me in regard to his course. But the trick worked against him rather than for him; when he came up he was nearer to me than before. I thought also that his strokes were growing weaker, and I was confirmed in such belief by the amount of water he splashed about, as if his efforts were desperate rather than judicious.

I swam, my strokes long and steady, and gained upon him with much rapidity. We were approaching the shore, when he, looking back, perceived that I must overtake him before he could reach land.

With an abruptness for which I was unprepared, he swam about and faced me as much as to say: " Come on; if you take me, you must fight me first."

Chudleigh, with only his head above water, was not especially beautiful to look at. The dirt with which he had disguised himself when he played false guide to us was washed off partly, and remained partly in streaks of mud, which made him look as if a hot gridiron had been slapped of a sudden upon his face. Moreover, Chudleigh was angry, very angry; his eyes snapped as if he were wondering why I could not let him alone.

I may have looked as ugly as Chudleigh, but I could not see for myself. I swam a little closer to him, looking him straight in the eye, in order that I might see what he intended to do the moment he thought it.

"Why do you follow me? " he asked, with much anger in his tone.

"Why do you run from me? " I asked.

"What I do is no business of yours," he said.

"Oh, yes, it is," I replied. "You're Captain Chudleigh of the British army, an escaped prissoner, and I've come to recapture you."

"I don't see how you're going to do it," he said.

"I do," I replied, though, to tell the truth, I had not yet thought of a way to manage the matter, which seemed to present difficulties. In the meantime I confined myself to treading water. Chudleigh did the same.

"That was a dirty trick you played on us back there," I said, "palming yourself off on us as a guide."

"I didn't do it," he replied in an injured tone. "You're to blame yourself. You forced me at the pistol's muzzle."

He told the truth, I was forced to confess.

"We'll let that pass," I said. "Now, will you surrender?"

"Never!" he replied, in manner most determined.

"Then you will force me to a violent recapture," I said.

"I fail to see how you are going to do it," he said with much grimness. "If you seize me here in the water, I will seize you, and then we will drown together, which will be very unpleasant for both of us."

There was much truth in what he said. A blind man or a fool could see it.

" Let us swim to land and fight it out with our fists," I proposed, remembering how I had overcome Albert, and confident that I could dispose of Chudleigh in similar fashion.

" Oh, no," he said decidedly, " I am very comfortable where I am."

" Then you like water better than most British officers," I said.

" It has its uses," he replied contentedly.

There was nothing more to do just then but to tread water and think.

" Come, come, captain," I said after a while, " be reasonable. I've overtaken you. You can't get away. Surrender like a gentleman, and let's go ashore and dry ourselves. This water's getting cold."

" I see no reason why I should surrender," he replied. " Besides, the water is no colder for you than it is for me."

There was no answer to this logic. Moreover, what he said sounded like a challenge. So I set myself to thinking with more concentra-

tion than ever. There was another and longer
interval of silence. I hoped that Whitestone
or Adams would appear, but neither did so.
After all, I had little right to expect either. We
had left them far behind, and also we had
changed our course. There was nothing to
guide them.

I addressed myself once more to Chudleigh's
reason.

"Your errand is at an end," I said.
"Whether I take you now or not, you can not
shake me off. You will never get through to
Clinton. Besides, you are losing all your pre-
cious time here in the river."

But he preserved an obstinacy most strange
and vexatious. He did not even reply to me,
but kept on treading water. I perceived that I
must use with him some other means than logic,
however sound and unanswerable the latter
might be.

Sometimes it happens to me, as doubtless
it does to other people, that after being long
in a puzzle, the answer comes to me so suddenly and so easily that I wonder why I did not
see it first glance.

Without any preliminaries that would seem

to warn Chudleigh, I dived out of sight. When
I came up I was in such shallow water that I
could wade. Near me was a huge bowlder pro-
truding a good two feet above the water. I
walked to it, climbed upon it, and taking a comfortable position above the water, looked at
Chudleigh, who seemed to be much surprised
and aggrieved at my sudden countermarch.

"What do you mean?" he asked.

"Nothing," I replied, "except that I am
tired of treading water. Come and join me;
it's very pleasant up here."

He declined my invitation, which I had
worded most courteously. I remained silent
for a while; then I said:

"Better come. You can't tread water forever. If you stay there much longer you'll
catch the cramp and drown."

I lolled on the bowlder and awaited the end
with calmness and satisfaction. My signal advantage was apparent.

"I'll swim to the other shore," said he presently.

"You can't," I replied. "It's too far; you
haven't strength enough left for it."

I could see that he was growing tired. He

looked around him at either shore and up and
down the river, but we were the only human
beings within the circle of that horizon.

"What terms of surrender do you pro-
pose?" he said at last, with a certain despair
in his tone.

"Unconditional."

"That is too hard."

"My advantage warrants the demand."

He was silent again for a few moments, and
was rapidly growing weaker. I thought I
would hasten matters.

"I will not treat you badly," I said. "All
I want to do is to take you back to our army."

"Well, I suppose I must accept," he said,
"for I am growing devilish cold and tired."

"Pledge your honor," I said, "that you
will make no attempt to escape, with the under-
standing that the pledge does not forbid
rescue."

"I give you my word," he said.

Whereupon he swam to shore, to the great
relief of us both.

CHAPTER XVI.

THE RETURN WITH CHUDLEIGH.

We climbed up the bank, and sat for some time drying in the sun. We were wet, and, moreover, had drunk large quantities of the Hudson River. As a regular thing, I prefer dry land as a place of inhabitation.

While the sun dried our bodies and clothing I was thinking. Though I had taken my man, and that, too, single-handed, my position was not the best in the world. I was now on the wrong side of the river, and I had lost my weapons and my comrades. Also I was hungry.

"Chudleigh," I asked, "are you hungry?'

"Rather," he replied with emphasis.

"How are we to get something to eat?" I asked.

"That's your affair, not mine," he replied. "I have nothing to do but to remain captured."

I thought I saw in him an inclination to be

disagreeable, which, to say the truth, was scarce
the part of a gentleman after the handsome
fashion in which I had treated him. In the face
of such ingratitude, I resolved to use the privi-
leges of my superior position.

"Are you about dry?" I asked.

"Yes."

"Then get up and march."

He seemed to resent my stern tone, but inasmuch as he had provoked it he had no cause
for complaint. If he intended to assert all the
rights of a prisoner, then I equally would assert
all the rights of a captor.

"Which way?" he asked.

"Northward, along the river bank. Keep
in front of me," I said.

Obedient to my orders he stalked off at a
pretty gait, and I followed. We marched thus
for half a mile. Chudleigh glanced back at me
once or twice. I seemed not to notice it, though
I could guess what was passing in his mind.

"If I hadn't given my word," he said, "I
think I'd fight it out with you, fist and skull."

"I offered you the chance," I said, "when
we were in the river, but you would not accept
it. You've heard many wise sayings about lost

opportunities, and this proves the truth of them."

"That's so," he said with a sigh of deep regret.

"Besides," I added, in the way of consolation for his lost opportunity, "you would gain nothing by it but bruises. I am larger and stronger than you."

He measured me with his eye and concluded that I spoke truth, for he heaved another sigh, but of comfort.

"Now, Chudleigh," I said, "a man can be a fool sometimes and lose nothing, but he can't be a fool all the time and gather the profits of the earth. Drop back here with me and let us talk and act sensibly."

He wrinkled his brow a moment or two, as if in thought, and accepted my invitation. Whereupon we became very good companions.

In reality I felt as much trouble about Chudleigh as myself. It was like the trouble I had felt on Albert's account. He had penetrated our lines in citizen's clothes, and if I took him back to our camp in the same attire he might be regarded as a spy, with all the unpleasant consequences such a thing entails. Having spared Chudleigh's life once from scruples, I had no mind to lead him to the gallows. I must get a British uniform for him, though how was more than I could tell. The problem troubled me much.

But the advance of hunger soon drove thoughts of Chudleigh's safety out of my mind, and, stubborn Englishman though he was, he was fain to confess that he too felt the desire for food. Along that side of the river the settlements were but scant, and nowhere did we see a house.

That we would encounter Whitestone and Adams was beyond all probability, for they would never surmise that we had crossed the river. Chudleigh and I looked ruefully and hungrily at each other.

" Chudleigh," I said, " you are more trouble a captive than a fugitive."

" The responsibility is yours," he said. " I decline to carry the burdens of my captor. Find me something to eat."

We trudged along for more than an hour, somewhat gloomy and the pains of hunger increasing. I was about to call a halt, that we might rest and that I might think about our difficulties, when I saw a column of smoke rising above a hill. I called Chudleigh's attention to it, and he agreed with me that we ought to push on and see what it was.

I was convinced that friends must be at the bottom of that column of smoke. If any British party had come so far north, which in itself was improbable, it could scarce be so careless as to give to the Americans plain warning of its presence.

It was a long walk, but we were cheered by the possibility that our reward would be dinner. Chudleigh seemed to cherish some lingering hope that it was a party of British or Tories who would rescue him, but I told him to save himself such disappointments.

In a short time we came in view of those who had built the fire, and I was delighted to find my surmise that they were Americans was correct.

They numbered some fifty or a hundred, and I guessed they were a detachment on the way to join the northern army beleaguering Burgoyne.

" Chudleigh," I said as we approached the

first sentinel, "will you promise to do all that
I say?"

"Of course; I am your prisoner," he replied.

I hailed the sentinel, and my uniform pro-
cured for me a friendly reception. Chudleigh
I introduced vaguely as a countryman traveling northward with me. The men were eat-
ing, and I told them we were making close
acquaintance with starvation. They invited us
to join them, and we fell to with great prompti-
tude.

I could tell them something about affairs at
the north, and they could give me the latest
news from the south. They told me that Clinton was still below Albany, hesitating and
awaiting with impatience some message from
Burgoyne.

I rejoiced more than ever that I had stopped
Chudleigh, and felt pride in my exploit. I hope
I can be pardoned for it. It was but natural
that Chudleigh's emotions should be the op-
posite of mine, and I watched his face to see
how he would take this talk. It was easy
enough to see regret expressed there, though
he sought to control himself.

The talk of these recruits was very bitter against the British. The Indians with Burgoyne had committed many cruel deeds before they fled back to Canada, and these countrymen were full of the passion for revenge. I often think that if the British in London knew what atrocities their red allies have committed in their wars with us they would understand more easily why so many of us are inflamed against the Englishman.

These men were rehearsing the latest murders by the Indians, and they showed very plainly their desire to arrive at the front before Burgoyne was taken. Nor did they spare the name of Englishman. I was sorry on Chudleigh's account that the talk had taken such drift. He took note of it from the first, because his red face grew redder, and he squirmed about in the manner which shows uneasiness.

"Chudleigh," I whispered at a moment when the others were not looking, "keep still. Remember you are my prisoner."

But he sat there swelling and puffing like an angry cat.

While the others were denouncing them, I made some excuses, most perfunctory, it is true,

for the British; but this was only an additional
incitement to a bellicose man named Hicks.
He damned the British for every crime known
to Satan. Chudleigh was so red in the face I
thought the blood would pop out through his
cheeks, and, though I shoved him warningly
with my boot, he blurted out his wrath.

"The English are as good as anybody, sir,
and you accuse them falsely!" he said.

"What is it to you?" exclaimed Hicks, turning to him in surprise and anger.

"I am an Englishman, sir," said Chudleigh
with ill-judged haughtiness, "and I will not endure such abuse."

"Oh, you are an Englishman, are you, and
you won't endure abuse, won't you?" said
Hicks with irony; and then to me, "We did not
understand you to say he was an Englishman."

I saw that we were in a pickle, and I thought
it best to tell the whole truth in a careless way,
as if the thing were but a trifle.

"The man is an English officer, an escaped
prisoner, whom I have retaken," I said. "I
did not deem it worth while to make long explanations, especially as we must now push on
after you have so kindly fed us."

But Hicks was suspicious; so were the others, and their suspicions were fed by the mutterings and growls of Chudleigh, who showed a lack of tact remarkable even in an Englishman out of his own country. Then, to appease them, I went into some of the long explanations which I had said I wanted to avoid.

" That's all very well," broke in Hicks, " but if this man is an English officer, why is he not in the English uniform?   I believe he is an Englishman, as you say; he talks like it, but tell me why he is dressed like a civilian."

The others followed Hicks's lead and began to cry:

"Spy! Spy! Spy!"

In truth I felt alarm.

" This is no spy," I said.   " He is Captain Chudleigh, of the English army."

" He may be Captain Chudleigh and a spy too," said Hicks coolly.   " I am not sure about the Chudleigh part, but I am about the spy part."

" Hang him for good count! " cried some of the others, who seemed to be raw recruits. The talk about the Indian atrocities was fresh in their minds, and they were in a highly inflammatory state. I recognized a real and present danger.

"Men," I cried, "you are going too far! This prisoner is mine, and it is of importance that I take him back to the army."

But my protest only seemed to excite them further. In truth they took it as a threat. Some of them began to demand that I too should be hung, that I was a Tory in disguise. But the body of them did not take up this cry. The bulk of their wrath fell upon Chudleigh, who was undeniably an Englishman. Two or three of the foremost made ready to seize him. I was in no mind to have all my plans spoiled, and I snatched a musket from a stack and threatened to shoot the first man who put a hand on Chudleigh.

Chudleigh himself behaved very well, and sat, quite calm. The men hesitated at sight of the rifle, and this gave me a chance to appeal to their reason, which was more accessible now since they seemed to be impressed by my earnestness. I insisted that all I had said was the truth, and they would be doing much injury to our cause if they interfered with us. I fancy that I pleaded our case with eloquence, though

I ought not to boast. At any rate they were mollified, and concluded to abandon their project of hanging Chudleigh.

"I've no doubt he deserves hanging," said Hicks, "but I guess we'll leave the job for somebody else."

Chudleigh was about to resent this, but I told him to shut up so abruptly that he forgot himself and obeyed.

I was anxious enough to be clear of these men, countrymen though they were; so we bade them adieu and tramped on, much strengthened by the rest and food.

"Captain," said I to Chudleigh, though trying to preserve a polite tone, "you do not seem to appreciate the beauty and virtue of silence."

"I will not have my country or my countrymen insulted," replied he in most belligerent tones.

"Well, at any rate," I said, "I had to save your life at the risk of my own."

"It was nothing more than your duty," he replied. "I am your prisoner, and you are responsible for my safety."

Which I call rank ingratitude on Chudleigh's part, though technically true.

It was late in the day when we met the detachment, and dark now being near at hand, it was apparent that we would have to sleep in the woods, which, however, was no hardship for soldiers, since the nights were warm and the ground dry. When the night arrived I proposed to Chudleigh that we stop and make our beds on the turf, which was rather thick and soft at that spot. He assented in the manner of one who had made up his mind to obey me in every particular.

But before lying down I had the forethought to ask from Chudleigh a guarantee that he would not walk away in the night while I was asleep. I reminded him of his pledge that he would not attempt to escape, barring a rescue.

But he took exceptions with great promptness, claiming with much plausibility, I was fain to admit, that his pledge did not apply in such a case. He argued that if I lay down and went to sleep he was no longer guarded; consequently he was not a prisoner; consequently he would go away. Since he chose to stick to his position, I had no way to drive him from it, whether reasonable or unreasonable.

"Then I will bind you hand and foot," I said.

He reminded me with an air of triumph that I had nothing with which to bind him, which unfortunately was true.

"What am I to do?" I said as much to myself as to him.

"Nothing that I can see," he replied, "but to guard me while I sleep."

Without another word he lay down upon the turf, and in less than two minutes his snore permeated the woods.

Reflecting in most unhappy fashion that if it were not for the great interests of our campaign I would much rather be his prisoner than have him mine, I sat there making fierce efforts to keep my eyelids apart.

CHAPTER XVII.

About midnight I reached the limit of endurance. I was firm in my resolution that I would not sleep, and while still firm in it I slept. When I awoke it was a fine day. For a moment I was in a cold terror, feeling sure Chudleigh had slipped away while I slept the sleep that had overpowered me. But a calm, evenly attuned snore that glided peacefully through the arches of the woods reassured me.

Chudleigh was lying on his back, sleeping. He was as heavy as a log, and I knew that he had not known a single waking moment since he lay down the night before. I dragged him about with rudeness and he opened his eyes regretfully. Presently he announced that he felt very fresh and strong, and asked me where I expected to get breakfast. He said he was

sorry for me, as he knew I must be very tired
and sleepy after sitting up on guard all night.

I gave him no answer, but commanded him
to resume the march with me. We walked on
with diligence through a breakfastless country.
Chudleigh, though suffering from hunger, was
frequent in his expressions of sympathy for me.
He said he had the utmost pity for any man
who was compelled to sit up an entire night
and watch prisoners; but I replied that I throve
upon it, and then Chudleigh showed chagrin.

We had the good fortune, about two hours
before noon, to find the house of a farmer, who
sold us some food, and cared not whether we
were American or British, Tory or nothing, so
long as we were good pay.

A half hour after leaving this place I decided
that we ought to recross the river. Chudleigh
offered no objection, knowing that he had no
right to do so, being a prisoner. I had no
mind to take another swim, so I made search
along the bank for something that would serve
as a raft, and was not long in finding it.

Having proved to Chudleigh that it was as
much to his benefit as to mine to help me, we
rolled a small tree that had fallen near the

water's edge into the river, and, sitting astride it, began our ride toward the farther shore. I had a pole with which I could direct the course of our raft, and with these aids it seemed rather an easy matter to cross. I allowed the tree to drift partly with the current, but all the time gently urged it toward the farther shore.

We floated along quite peacefully. So far as we could see we were alone upon the broad surface of the river, and the shores too were deserted. I remarked upon the loneliness of it all to Chudleigh, and he seemed impressed.

"Chudleigh," I said, "we're having an easier time recrossing the river than we had crossing it."

"So it would seem," he replied, "but we won't unless you look out for the current and those rocks there."

I had twisted my face about while speaking to Chudleigh, and in consequence neglected the outlook ahead. We had reached a shallow place in the river where some sharp rocks stuck up, and the water eddied about them in manner most spirited. The front end of our log was caught in one of these eddies and whirled about with violence. I was thrown off, and though I grasped at the log it slipped away from me. I whirled about to recover myself, but the fierce current picked me up and dashed me against one of the projecting rocks. With a backward twist I was able to save myself a little, but my head struck the cruel stone with grievous force.

I saw many stars appear suddenly in the full day. Chudleigh and the log vanished, and I was drifting away through the atmosphere. I was not wholly unconscious, and through the instinct of an old swimmer made some motions which kept me afloat a little while with the current.

I had too little mind left to command my nerves and muscles, but enough to know that I was very near death. In a dazed and bewildered sort of way I expected the end, and was loath to meet it.

The blue sky was rapidly fading into noth-ing, when some voice from a point a thousand miles away called to me to hold up a little longer. The voice was so sharp and imperious that it acted like a tonic upon me, and brain resumed a little control over body. I tried to

16

swim, but I was too weak to do more than paddle a little. The voice shouted again, and encouraged me to persevere.

In truth I tried to persevere, but things were whizzing about so much in my head and I was so weak that I could do but little. I thought I was bound to go down, with the whole river pouring into my ears.

"That's a good fellow!" shouted the voice. "Hold up just a minute longer, and I'll have you safe!"

I saw dimly a huge figure bearing down upon me. It reached out and grasped me by the collar.

"Steady, now!" continued the voice. "Here comes our tree, and we'll be safe in twenty seconds!"

The tree, looking like a mountain, floated down toward us. My rescuer reached out, seized it, and then dragged us both upon it. Reposing in safety, mind and strength returned, and things resumed their natural size and shape. Chudleigh, the Hudson River running in little cascades from his hair down his face, was sitting firmly astride the log and looking at me with an air of satisfaction.

"Chudleigh," I said, "I believe you have saved my life."

"Shelby," he replied, "I know it."

"Why didn't you escape?" I asked.

"You compel me to remind you that I am a gentleman, Mr. Shelby," he said.

That was all that ever passed between us on the subject, though I reflected that I was not in his debt, for if he had saved my life I had saved his.

We had no further difficulty in reaching the desired shore, where the sun soon dried us. We continued our journey in very amicable fashion, Chudleigh no doubt feeling relief because he was now in a measure on even terms with me. I, too, was in a state of satisfaction. Unless Burgoyne had retreated very fast, we could not now be far from the lines of the American army, and I thought that my troubles with my prisoner were almost at an end. I hoped that Burgoyne had not been taken in my absence, for I wished to be present at the taking. I also had in my mind another plan with which Chudleigh was concerned. It was a plan of great self-sacrifice, and I felt the virtuous glow which arises from such resolutions.

We paused again, by and by, for rest, the sun having become warm and the way dusty. Chudleigh sat down on a stone and wiped his damp face, while I went to a brook, which I had seen glimmering among the trees, for a drink of fresh water. I had just knelt down to drink when I heard a clattering of hoofs. Rising hastily, I saw two men riding toward Chudleigh. Though the faces of these two men were much smeared with dust, I recognized them readily and joyfully. They were Whitestone and Adams.

My two comrades evidently had seen and recognized Chudleigh. They raised a shout and galloped toward him as if they feared he would flee. I came down to the edge of the wood and stopped there to see at my leisure what might happen.

Chudleigh sat upon the stone unmoved. As a matter of course he both saw and heard Whitestone and Adams, but he was a phlegmatic sort of fellow and took no notice. Whitestone reached him first. Leaping from his horse, the gallant sergeant exclaimed:

" Do you surrender, captain? "

" Certainly," said Chudleigh.

" It's been a long chase, captain, but we've got you at last," continued the sergeant.

" So it seems," said Chudleigh, with the same phlegm.

Then I came from the wood and cut the sergeant's comb for him; but he was so glad to see me again that he was quite willing to lose the glory of the recapture. He explained that he had been overtaken by Adams. Together they had wandered around in search of Chudleigh and me. Giving up the hunt as useless, they had obtained new horses and were on the way back to the army.

We were now four men and two horses, and the men taking turns on horseback, we increased our speed greatly.

Whitestone and Adams were in fine feather, but there was one question that yet bothered me. I wanted to take Chudleigh back in his own proper British uniform, and thus save him from unpleasant possibilities. I did not see how it could be done, but luck helped me.

We met very soon a small party of Americans escorting some British prisoners. Telling my companions to wait for me, I approached the sergeant who was in charge of the troop.

Making my manner as important as I could, and speaking in a low tone, as if fearful that I would be overheard—which I observe always impresses people—I told him that one of our number was about to undertake a most delicate and dangerous mission. It chanced that I had some slight acquaintance with this sergeant, and therefore he had no reason to doubt my words, even if I am forced to say it myself.

He pricked up his ears at once, all curiosity, and wanted to know the nature of the business. I pointed to Chudleigh, who was standing some distance away with Whitestone and Adams, and said he was going to enter the British lines as a spy in order to procure most important information.

"A dangerous business, you say truly. He must be a daring fellow," said my man, nodding his head in the direction of Chudleigh.

"So he is," I said, "ready at any moment to risk his life for the cause, but we need one thing."

He asked what it was.

"A disguise," I said. "If he is to play the British soldier, of course he must have a British soldier's clothes."

I made no request, but I looked suggestive-
ly at the British prisoners. The sergeant, who
was all for obliging me, took the hint at once.
He picked out the very best uniform in the lot,
and made the man who wore it exchange it for
Chudleigh's old clothes. Chudleigh, who had
been learning wisdom in the last day or two,
was considerate enough to keep his mouth shut,
and we parted from the sergeant and his troop
with many mutual expressions of good will.
The uniform did not fit Chudleigh, nor was it
that of an officer, but these were minor details
to which no attention would be paid in the press
of a great campaign.

The matter of the uniform disposed of, we
pressed forward with renewed spirit, and soon
reached the first, sentinels of our army, which
we found surrounding that of Burgoyne. It
was with great satisfaction that I delivered
Chudleigh to my colonel.

The colonel was delighted at the recapture,
and praised me with such freedom that I began
to have a budding suspicion that I ought to be
commander in chief of the army. However, I
made no mention of the suspicion. Instead,
I suggested to the colonel that as Chudleigh

had escaped once, he might escape again, and it would be well to exchange him for some officer of ours whom the British held.

The colonel took to the idea, and said he would speak to the general about it. In the morning he told me it would be done, and I immediately asked him for the favor of taking Chudleigh into the British camp, saying that as I had been his jailer so much already, I would like to continue in that capacity until the end.

The colonel was in great good humor with me, and he granted the request forthwith. As I left to carry out the business, he said, " The exchange is well enough, but we'll probably have your man back in a few days."

In truth it did look rather odd that the British should be exchanging prisoners with us upon what we regarded as the unavoidable eve of their surrender, but they chose to persevere in the idea that we were yet equal enemies. Nevertheless, the coils of our army were steadily tightening around them. All the fords were held by our troops. Our best sharpshooters swept the British camp, and it is no abuse of metaphor to say that Burgoyne's army was rimmed around by a circle of fire.

I found Chudleigh reposing under a tree, and told him to get up and start with me at once.

. " What new expedition is this? " he asked discontentedly. " Can not I be permitted to rest a little? I will not try to escape again? "

I told him he was about to be exchanged, and I had secured the privilege of escorting him back to his own people.

" That's very polite of you," he said.

I really believe he thought so.

For the second time I entered Burgoyne's camp under a white flag, and saw all the signs of distress I had seen before, only in a sharper and deeper form. The wounded and sick were more numerous and the well and strong were fewer. It was a sorely stricken army.

But I did not waste much time in such observations, which of necessity would have been but limited anyhow, as the British had no intent to let any American wander at will about their camp and take note of their situation. When we were halted at the outskirts, I asked the officer who received us for Albert Van Auken, who, I said, was a friend of mine and of whose safety I wished to be assured. He was

very courteous, and in a few minutes Albert
came.

Albert was glad to see me, and I to see him,
and as soon as we had shaken hands I approached the matter I had in mind.

"Madame Van Auken, your mother, and
your sister, are they well, Albert?" I asked.

"Very well, the circumstances considered,"
replied Albert, "though I must say their quarters are rather restricted.   You can see the
house up there; they have been living for the
last three or four days and nights in its cellar,
crowded up with other women, with a hospital
beside them, and the cannon balls from your
army often crashing over their heads.   It's
rather a lively life for women."

"Can't I see your sister, Mistress Catherine?" I asked.   "I have something to say to
her about Chudleigh."

"Why, certainly," he replied.   "Kate will
always be glad to see an old playmate like you,
Dick."

He was so obliging as to go at once and
fetch her. She looked a little thin and touched
by care, but the added gravity became her. She
greeted me with gratifying warmth. We had

stepped a little to one side, and after the greet-
ings, I said, indicating Chudleigh:

"I have brought him back as sound and
whole as he was the day he started on this
campaign."

"That must be very pleasant to Captain
Chudleigh," she said with a faint smile.

"I saved him from a possible death too,"
I said.

"Captain Chudleigh's debt of gratitude to
you is large," she replied.

"I have taken great trouble with him," I
said, "but I was willing to do it all on your
account. I have brought him back, and I make
him a present to you."

She looked me squarely in the eyes for a
moment, and said, as she turned away:

"Dick, you are a fool!"

Which I call abrupt, impolite, ungrateful,
and, I hope, untrue.

CHAPTER XVIII.

THE BATTLE OF THE GUNS.

I returned to our camp downcast over the failure of good intentions, and convinced that there was no reward in this life for self-sacrifice. Perhaps if I were to fall in the fighting and Kate Van Auken were to see my dead body, she would be sorry she had called me a fool. There was comfort in this reflection. The idea that I was a martyr cheered me, and I recovered with a rapidity that was astonishing to myself.

An hour's rest was permitted me before my return to active duty, and I had some opportunity to observe our tactics, which I concluded must be most galling to the enemy. Some clouds of smoke hung over both encampments, and the crackling of the rifles of the sharpshooters and the occasional thud of the cannon had become so much a matter of course, that we scarce paid attention to them.

When my hour of leisure was over I was assigned to duty with an advanced party close up to Burgoyne's camp. It was much to my pleasure that I found Whitestone there too. It was but natural, however, that we should be often on duty together, since we belonged to the same company.

Whitestone, according to his habit, had made himself comfortable on the ground, and, there being no law against it, was smoking the beloved pipe, which like its master was a veteran of many campaigns. From his lounging place he could see a portion of the British camp.

"Mr. Shelby," said he, "this is like sitting by and watching a wounded bear die, and giving him a little prod now and then to hurry the death along."

So it was, and it was no wonder the soldiers grew impatient. But I was bound to confess that the policy of our generals was right, and by it they would win as much and save more life.

There was nothing for me to do, and I kept my eyes most of the time on the house Albert had pointed out to me. Crouched in its cellar

I knew were scared women and weeping children, and doubtless Kate and her mother were among them. Once a cannon ball struck the house and went through it, burying itself in the ground on the other side. I held my breath for a little, but I was reassured by the thought that the women and children were out of range in the cellar.

Thus the day passed in idleness as far as I was concerned. I spent it not unpleasantly in gossip with Whitestone. The nightfall was dark, and under cover of it the British ran a twenty-four pounder forward into a good position and opened fire with it upon some of our advanced parties. My first warning of the attack was a loud report much nearer to us than usual, followed by a hissing and singing as if something were stinging the air, and then a solid chunk of iron struck the earth with a vengeful swish a few yards from us. A cloud of dirt was spattered in our faces, stinging us like bees.

When we had recovered from our surprise, and assured ourselves we were neither dead nor dying, we made remarks about chance, and the probability that no other cannon ball would

strike near us during the campaign. Just as
the last of such remarks were spoken we heard
the roar and heavy boom, followed by the rapid
swish through the air, and the cannon ball
struck a full yard nearer to us than the first.
We used vigorous and, I fear, bad language,
which, however, is a great relief sometimes, especially to a soldier.

"They've pushed that gun up too close to
us," said Whitestone. "It's among those trees
across there. The darkness has helped them."

We were of opinion that the men with the
gun had our range—that is, of our particular
party—and we thought it wise and healthy to
lie down and expose the least possible surface.
I awaited the third shot with much curiosity
and some apprehension.

Presently we saw a twinkle, as of a powder
match, and then a great flash. The ball shrieked
through the air, and with a shiver that could
not be checked we waited for it to strike. True
to its predecessors, it followed nearly the same
course and smashed against a stone near us.
One of our men was struck by the rebounding
of fragments, of iron or stone, and severely
wounded. It was too dark to see well, but his

groans spoke for him. Whitestone and I took hold of him and carried him back for treatment. While we were gone, one man was slain and another wounded in the same way. In the darkness that British cannon had become a live thing and was stinging us. Some of our best sharpshooters were chosen to slay the cannoneers, but they could aim only by the flash of the gun, and the men loading it had the woods to protect them. The bullets were wasted, and the troublesome hornet stung again and again.

We were perplexed. Our pride as well as our safety was concerned. The idea came to me at last.

"To fight fire with fire is an old saying," I remarked to Whitestone.

"What do you mean?" he asked.

"Why, we must have a cannon too," I said.

He understood at once, for Whitestone is not a dull man. He volunteered to get the cannon and I went along with him to help. We presented our claim with such urgency and eloquence that the artillery officer to whom we went was impressed. Also he was near enough to see how damaging and dangerous the British cannon had become.

"You can have Old Ty," he said, "and be sure you make good use of him."

I did not understand, but Whitestone did. He knew Old Ty. He explained that Old Ty, which was short for "Old Ticonderoga," was a twenty-four pounder taken at Ticonderoga early in the war by Ethan Allen and his Green Mountain Boys. It had done so much service and in so many campaigns that the gunners had affectionately nicknamed the veteran Old Ty in memory of the fortress in which he had been taken.

"I've seen Old Ty," said Whitestone. "He's been battered about a good lot, but he's got a mighty bad bark and a worse bite."

In a few minutes the groaning of wheels and the shout of the driver to the horses announced the approach of Old Ty. I stood aside with respect while the gun passed, and a grim and fierce old veteran he was, full worthy the respect of a youngster such as I felt myself to be.

Old Ty was of very dark metal, and there were many scars upon him where he had received the blows of enemies of a like caliber.

17

A wheel which had been struck by a ball in the heat of action was bent a trifle to one side, and Old Ty rolled along as if he were a little lame and didn't mind it. His big black muzzle grinned at me as if he were proud of his scars, and felt good for many more.

Just behind the gun walked a man as ugly and battered as Old Ty himself.

"That's Goss, the gunner," said Whitestone. "He's been with Old Ty all through the war, and loves him better than his wife."

On went the fierce and ugly pair like two who knew their duty and loved it.

The night, as usual after the first rush of darkness, had begun to brighten a bit. We could see the British cannon, a long, ugly piece, without waiting for its flash; yet its gunners were protected so well by fresh-felled trees and a swell of the earth that our sharpshooters could not pick them off. They were in good position, and nothing lighter than Old Ty could drive them out of it.

The British saw what we were about and sought to check us. They fired more rapidly, and a cannon ball smashed one of the horses hitched to Old Ty almost to a pulp. But

Goss sprang forward, seized one wheel, and threw the veteran into place.

Old Ty had a position much like that of his antagonist, and Goss, stroking his iron comrade like one who pets an old friend, began to seek the range, and take very long and careful looks at the enemy. Lights along the line of either army flared up, and many looked on.

" Lie flat on the ground here," said Whitestone to me. " This is going to be a pitched battle between the big guns, and you want to look out."

I adopted Whitestone's advice, thinking it very good. Old Ty's big black muzzle grinned threateningly across at his antagonist, as if he longed to show his teeth, but waited the word and hand of his comrade.

" There goes the bark of the other! " cried Whitestone.

The bright blaze sprang up, the British cannon roared, and hurled his shot. The mass of iron swept over Old Ty and buried itself in the hillside.

" Much bark, but no bite," said Whitestone.

Old Ty, black and defiant, was yet silent.

Goss was not a man who hurried himself or his comrade. We waited, breathless. Suddenly Goss leaned over and touched the match.

Old Ty spoke in the hoarse, roaring voice that indicates much wear. One of the felled trees in the British position was shattered, and the ball bounded to the right and was lost to sight.

"A little bite," said Whitestone, "but not deep enough."

Old Ty smoked and grew blacker, as if he were not satisfied with himself. They swabbed out his mouth and filled it with iron again.

Where I lay I could see the muzzles of both cannon threatening each other. The Briton was slower than before, as if he wished to be sure. Goss continued to pat his comrade by way of stirring up his spirit. That did not seem to me to be needed, for Old Ty was the very fellow I would have chosen for such a furious contention as this.

The two champions spoke at the same instant, and the roar of them was so great that for the moment I thought I would be struck deaf. A great cloud of smoke enveloped either cannon, but when it raised both sides cheered.

Old Ty had received a fresh blow on his lame wheel, and careened a little farther to one side, but the Briton was hit the harder of the two. His axle had been battered by Old Ty's ball, and the British were as busy as bees propping him up for the third raid.

" Rather evenly matched," grunted White-stone, " and both full of grit. I think we shall have some very pretty sport here."

I was of Whitestone's opinion.

I could see Goss frowning. He did not like the wound Old Ty had received, and stroked the lame wheel. " Steady, old partner," I heard him say. " We'll beat 'em yet."

All at once I noticed that the lights along the line had increased, and some thousands were looking on at the battle of the two giants.

" Old Ty must win! " I said to Whitestone. " We can't let him lose."

" I don't know," said Whitestone, shaking his head. " A battle's never over till the last shot's fired."

The Briton was first, and it was well that we were sheltered. The ball glanced along Old

Ty's barrel, making a long rip in the iron, and bounded over our heads and across the hill.

" Old Ty got it that time," said Whitestone. " That was a cruel blow."

He spoke truth, and a less seasoned veteran than Old Ty would have been crushed by it. There was a look of deep concern on Goss's face as he ran his hand over the huge rent in Old Ty's side. Then his face brightened a bit, and I concluded the veteran was good for more hard blows.

The blow must have had some effect upon Old Ty's voice or temper. At any rate, when he replied his roar was hoarser and angrier. A cry arose from the British ranks, and I saw them taking away a body. Old Ty had tasted blood. But the British cannon was as formidable as ever.

" The chances look a bit against Old Ty," commented Whitestone, and I had to confess to myself, although with reluctance, that it was so.

Goss was very slow in his preparations for the fourth shot. He had the men to steady Old Ty, and he made a slight change in the elevation. Again both spoke at the same time, and Old Ty groaned aloud as the mass of British iron tore along his barrel, ripping out a gap deeper and longer than any other. His own bolt tore off one of the Briton's wheels.

" The Englishman's on one leg," said White-stone, " but Old Ty's got it next to the heart. Chances two to one in favor of the English-man."

I sighed.   Poor Old Ty!   I could not bear to see the veteran beaten.   Goss's hard, dark face showed grief. He examined Old Ty with care and fumbled about him.

" What is he doing? " I asked of White-stone, who lay nearer the gun.

" I think he's trying to see if Old Ty will stand another shot," he said. " He's got some big rips in the barrel, and he may leave in all directions when the powder explodes."

Old Ty in truth was ragged and torn like a veteran in his last fight. The Briton had lost one wheel and was propped up on the side, but his black muzzle looked triumphant across the way.

The British fired again and then shouted

in triumph.   Old Ty, too, had lost a wheel,
which the shot had pounded into old iron.

" Old Ty is near his end," said Whitestone. " One leg gone and holes in his body
as big as my hat; that's too much! "

Old Ty was straightened up, and Goss
giving the word, the shot was rolled into his
wide mouth.   Then the gunner, as grim and
battered as his gun, took aim.   Upon the instant all our men rushed to cover.

Goss touched the match, and a crash far out-
doing all the others stunned us.   With the noise
in my ears and the smoke in my eyes I knew not
what had happened.   But Whitestone cried
aloud in joy.   Rubbing my eyes clear, I looked
across to see the effect of the shot.   I saw only
a heap of rubbish.   Old Ty's bolt had smote
his enemy and blown up the caisson and the
cannon with it.

Then I looked at Old Ty to see how he
bore his triumph, but his mighty barrel was
split asunder and he was a cannon no longer,
just pieces of old iron.

Sitting on a log was some one with tears on
his hard, brown face.   It was Goss, the gunner,
weeping over the end of his comrade.

CHAPTER XIX.

THE MAN FROM CLINTON.

At one o'clock in the morning I went off duty, and at five minutes past one o'clock I had begun a very pleasant and healthful slumber. At eight o'clock I awoke, and found Whitestone sitting by a little fire cooking strips of bacon, some of which he was so kind as to give me.

Whitestone's face was puffed out in the manner of one who has news to tell, and I was quite willing that he should gratify himself by telling it to me.

" What is it, Whitestone? " I asked. " Has the British army surrendered while I slept? "

" No," said Whitestone, " and it may not surrender after all."

" What! " I exclaimed.

" It's just as I say," said Whitestone, lighting the inevitable pipe. " It may not surrender after all."

" What has happened? "

Whitestone's cheeks continued to swell with a sense of importance.

" Clinton's advancing with seven thousand men," he said.

" That's nothing," I said. " Clinton's been advancing for weeks, and he never gets near us."

" But he is near us this time, sure enough," said the sergeant very seriously.

I was still unbelieving, and looked my unbelief.

" It's as I say," resumed the sergeant; " there is no doubt about it. Just after daylight this morning some skirmishers took a messenger from Clinton, who bore dispatches announcing his arrival within a very short time. It seems that Clinton is much farther up the river than we supposed, and that his army is also much larger than all our reckonings made it. I guess that with re-enforcements he got over the fright we gave him."

This in truth sounded like a matter of moment. I asked Whitestone if he was sure of what he reported, and he said the news was all

over the camp. I must confess that I felt as if
it were a personal blow. I had looked upon the
capture of Burgoyne as a certainty, but the
arrival of Clinton with seven thousand fresh
men would be sure to snatch the prize from us.
It looked like a very jest of fate that we should
lose our spoil after all our labors and battles.

"What's to be done, Whitestone?" I asked
gloomily.

"In a case of this kind," he replied, "I'm
glad that I'm a humble sergeant, and not a general. Let the generals settle it. Take another
piece of the bacon; it's crisp and fresh."

"Have you seen this captured messenger?"
I asked.

"No," replied Whitestone. "They have
. him in a tent over yonder, and I think the
officers have been busy with him, trying to
pump him."

As soon as I finished the bacon I walked
about the camp to see if I could learn anything
further concerning the matter, in which attempt
I failed. I saw, however, its effect upon the
army, which vented its feelings largely in the way
of swearing. The soldiers expected we would
have to leave Burgoyne and turn southward to

fight Clinton. Some said luck was always against us.

I was interrupted in my stroll by a message from my colonel to come at once. I hurried to him with some apprehension. He had expressed his high confidence in me of late, and, as I have said before, these high confidences bring hard duties.

But the matter was not so difficult as I had expected.

"Mr. Shelby," said the colonel, "we took prisoner this morning a man bearing important dispatches from Clinton to Burgoyne—you have heard about it, doubtless; it seems to be known all over the camp—and I am directly responsible for his safe keeping for the time being. He is in that tent which you can see on the hillside. Take three men and guard him. You need not intrude upon him, though; he seems to be a very gentlemanly fellow."

Of course I chose Whitestone as one of my three men, and we began our guard over the tent. I understood from the gossip Whitestone had picked up that the generals were debating what movement to make after the important news obtained, and probably they would examine the prisoner again later on. It was not at all likely that the prisoner, placed as he was in the center of our camp, could escape, but there might be reasons for keeping him close in the tent; so our watch was very strict.

Nevertheless, Whitestone and I chatted a bit, which was within our right, and tried to guess what would be the result of the campaign if we had to turn southward and fight Clinton, with Burgoyne on our rear. Doubtless some of these comments and queries were heard by the prisoner, whose feet I could see sticking out in front of the tent flap, but whose body was beyond our view. But I did not see that it mattered, and we talked on with freedom. Once I saw the prisoner's feet bob up a bit, as if he suffered from some kind of nervous contraction, but I made very slight note of it.

The debate of the generals lasted long, and I inferred, therefore, that their perplexity was great. Whitestone and I ceased to talk, and as I, having command of the little detachment, was under no obligation to parade, musket on shoulder, I sat down on a stone near the flap of the tent and made myself as comfortable as I could. From my position I could still see the prisoner's boots, a substantial British pair, of a kind that we could envy, for most of the time we were nearly bare of foot, sometimes entirely so.

The camp was peaceful, on the whole. The rattle of drums, the sound of voices, rose in the regular, steady fashion which becomes a hum. The prisoner was silent—unusually silent. He seemed to have no curiosity about us, and to prefer to remain in the shadow of his tent. In his place, I would have had my head out looking at everything. I noticed presently the attitude of his boots. They were cocked up on their heels, toes high in the air. I inferred immediately that the man was lying flat on his back, which was not at all unreasonable, as he probably needed rest after traveling all night.

The hum of the camp became a murmur, and it was answered by a slighter murmur from the tent. The prisoner was snoring. He was not only flat upon his back, but asleep. I felt an admiration for the calmness of mind which could turn placidly to slumber in such an exciting situation. A curiosity about this prisoner, already born in me, began to grow. He was most likely a man worth knowing.

I concluded that I would take a look at the
sleeping Englishman despite my orders. I did
not mention my idea to Whitestone, because
I thought he might object, and hint it was
none of my business to go in. I stooped down
and entered the tent, which was a small
one. As I surmised, the prisoner was lying
upon his back and was fast asleep. The
snore, which became much more assertive
now that I had entered the tent, left no doubt
about his slumbers. Yet I could not see his
face, which was far back under the edge of the
tent.

I reached back and pulled the tent-flap still
farther aside, letting in a fine flow of sunlight.
It fell directly upon the face of the prisoner,
bringing out every feature with the distinct-
ness of carving.

My first emotion was surprise; my second,
wrath; my third, amusement.

The prisoner was Albert Van Auken.

I do not claim that mine is the acutest mind
in the world; but at a single glance I saw to
the bottom of the whole affair, and the desire
to laugh grew very strong upon me. It had
not been twenty-four hours since I was talk-

ing to Albert Van Auken in Burgoyne's camp,
and here he was a prisoner in our camp, bringing dispatches from Clinton, down the river, to
Burgoyne.   I believe some things—not all
things.

I perceived that the bright light shining
directly into Albert's eyes would soon awaken
him.   In truth he was yawning even then.   I
sat down in front of him, closing my arms
around my knees in the attitude of one who
waits.

Albert yawned prodigiously.   I guessed that
he must have been up all the previous night
to have become so sleepy.   He would have relapsed into slumber, but the penetrating streak
of sunshine would not let him.   It played all
over his face, and inserting itself between his
eyelids, pried them open.

Albert sat up, and, after the manner of man,
rubbed his eyes.   He knew that some one was
in the tent with him, but he could not see who
it was.   I had taken care of that.   I was in the
dark and he was in the light.

"Well, what is it you wish?" he asked, after
he had finished rubbing his eyes.

I guessed that he took me for one of the

general officers who had been examining him. I have a trick of changing my voice when I wish to do so, and this was one of the times when I wished.

" I am to ask you some further questions in regard to the matters we were discussing this morning," I said.

" Well! " said Albert impatiently, as if he would like to be done with it.

" According to the dispatches which we secured when we took you," I said, " Sir Henry Clinton was very near at hand with a large army."

" Certainly," said Albert, in a tone of great emphasis.

" It is strange," I said, " that we did not hear of his near approach until we took you this morning. Our scouts and skirmishers have brought us no such news."

" It is probably due to the fact, general," said Albert politely, " that we captured your scouts and skirmishers as we advanced northward. Our celerity of movement was so great that they could not escape us."

" That was remarkable marching, in truth," I said admiringly. " You Englishmen are as

18

rapid in movement as you are strenuous in battle."

"Thank you, general," said Albert, with complacent vanity. I felt a strong inclination to kick him. I hate Tories, and, in particular, those who would have people think they are Englishmen.

"I believe you said Sir Henry Clinton had several thousand men with him," I resumed.

"I did not say it," replied Albert, "but most unfortunately it was revealed in the dispatches which you captured upon me. I may add, however, that the number is nearer eight thousand than seven thousand."

I understood the impression he wished to create, and I was willing to further his humor.

"Eight thousand with Sir Henry Clinton," I said, as if musing, "and Burgoyne has six thousand; that makes fourteen thousand, all regular troops, thoroughly armed and equipped otherwise. We can scarce hope to capture both armies."

"Not both, nor one either," said Albert in derision. "As a matter of fact, general, I think you will have some difficulty in looking after your own safety."

"By what manner of reasoning do you arrive at that conclusion?" asked I, wishing to lead him on.

"Oh, well, you know what British troops are," said Albert superciliously; "and when fourteen thousand of them are together, I imagine that troubles have arrived for · their enemies."

My inclination to kick him took on a sudden and violent increase. It was with the most extreme difficulty that I retained command over my mutinous foot.

"Perhaps it is as you assert," I said musingly. "In fact there would seem to be no doubt that it is best for us to let Burgoyne go, and retreat with what rapidity we can."

"Of course! of course!" said Albert eagerly. "That is the only thing you can do."

Now a desire to laugh instead of a desire to kick overspread me; but I mastered it as I had the other.

"I wish to tell you, however," I said, assuming my politest manner, "and in telling you I speak for the other American generals, that however little we are pleased with the news you bear, we are much pleased with the bearer. We have found you to be a young gentleman of courtesy, breeding, and discernment."

"Thank you," said Albert in a tone of much gratification.

"And," I resumed, "we have arrived at a certain conclusion; I may add also that we have arrived at that conclusion quickly and unanimously."

"What is it?" asked Albert with eager interest.

"That we have met many graceful and accomplished liars in our time, but of them all you are the most graceful and accomplished," I said with grave politeness, my tongue lingering over the long words.

Albert uttered something which sounded painfully and amazingly like an oath, and sprang to his feet, his face flushing red with anger or shame, I am uncertain which.

He raised his hand as if he would strike me, but I moved around a little, and the light in its turn fell on my face. He uttered another cry, and this time there was no doubt about its being an oath. He looked at me, his face growing redder and redder.

"Dick," he said in a tone of deep reproach, "I call this devilish unkind."

"The unkindness is all on your side, Albert," I retorted. "You have given me more trouble in this campaign than all the rest of Burgoyne's army—if that fellow Chudleigh be counted out —and here I have you on my hands again."

"Who asked you to come into my tent?" said Albert angrily. "I heard you outside a while ago, but I did not think you would come in."

"That was when your feet bobbed up," I said. "You must retain more control over them, Albert. Now that I think of it, and trace things to their remote causes, that movement first stirred in me the curiosity to see your face, and not your feet only. Have them amputated, Albert."

"What do you mean to do?" he asked with an air of resignation.

"Mean to do!" I said in a tone of surprise. "Why, I mean to retreat with all the remainder of our army as quickly as we can in order to get out of the way of those fourteen thousand invincible British veterans who will soon be united in one force."

"Now stop that, Dick," said Albert en-
treatingly. "Don't be too hard on a fellow."

"All right," I replied; "go to sleep again."

Without further ado I left the tent, and
found Whitestone waiting outside in some
anxiety.

"You stayed so long," he said, "I thought
perhaps the fellow had killed you."

"Not by any means as bad as that," I replied. "I found him to be a very pleasant
young man, and we had a conversation long
and most interesting."

"About what?" Whitestone could not keep
from asking.

"About many things," I replied, "and one
thing that I learned was of special importance."

"What was that?"

"How to send Clinton and his eight thousand men back below Albany, hold Burgoyne
fast, and continue the campaign as it was begun."

"That's a pretty big job," said Whitestone,
"for one man, and that one, too, rather young
and not overweighted with rank."

"Maybe you think so," I said with lofty indifference. "But I can do it, and, what is more,

I will prove to you that I can. You can stay here while I go down to the council of generals and tell them what to do."

Not giving Whitestone time to recover, I stalked off in a state of extreme dignity.

CHAPTER XX.

I pressed into the council of the generals with an energy that would not be denied, also with some strength of the knee, as an officious aid-de-camp can testify even at this late day. As a matter of course, my information was of such quality that everybody was delighted with me and praise became common. Again I felt as if I ought to be commander in chief. Again I had sufficient self-sacrifice to keep the thought to myself.

As I left the room they were talking about the disposition of the prisoner who had tried to trick us into precipitate flight and the abandonment of our prey. This put an idea into my head, and I told it to a colonel near the door, who in his turn told it to their high mightinesses, the generals, who were wise

274

enough to approve of it, and, in truth, to indorse it most heartily.

I suggested that Albert be sent back to Burgoyne with the most gracious compliments of our commander in chief, who was pleased to hear the news of the speedy arrival of Clinton, which would greatly increase the number of prisoners we were about to take. I asked, as some small reward for my great services, that I be chosen to escort Albert into the British camp and deliver the message. That, too, was granted readily.

"You can deliver the message by word of mouth," said one of the generals; "it would be too cruel a jest to put it in writing, and perhaps our dignity would suffer also."

I was not thinking so much of the jest as of another plan I had in mind.

I found Whitestone keeping faithful watch at the tent.

"Well," said he, with a croak that he meant for a laugh of sarcasm, "I suppose the generals fell on your neck and embraced you with delight when you told them what to do."

"They did not fall on my neck, but certainly they were very much delighted," I said;

"and they are going to do everything I told them to do."

"That's right," said Whitestone. "Keep it up. While you're spinning a yarn, spin a good one."

"It's just as I say," I said, "and as the first proof of it, I am going to take the prisoner as a present to Burgoyne."

Turning my back on the worthy sergeant, I entered the tent, and found Albert reclining on a blanket, the expression of chagrin still on his face. To tell the truth, I did not feel at all sorry for him, for, as I have said before, Albert had been a great care to me.

"Get up," I said with a roughness intended, "and come with me."

"What are they going to do with me?" asked Albert. "They can't hang me as a spy; I was taken in full uniform."

"Nobody wants to hang you, or do you any other harm," I said. "In your present lively and healthful condition you afford us too much amusement. We do not see how either army could spare you. Put your hat on and come on."

He followed very obediently and said nothing. He knew I held the whip hand over him.

"Sergeant," I said to Whitestone, "you need not watch any longer, since the tent is empty."

Then I took Albert away without another word. I had it in mind to punish Whitestone, who was presuming a little on his age and experience and his services to me.

I really could not help laughing to myself as I went along. This would make the third time I had entered Burgoyne's camp as an escort—once with Chudleigh, once with Albert's sister and mother, and now with Albert. I was fast getting to be at home in either camp. I began to feel a bit of regret at the prospect of Burgoyne's speedy surrender, which would break up all these pleasant little excursions.

Albert showed surprise when he saw us leaving our camp and going toward Burgoyne's.

"What are you going to do?" he asked.

"Nothing, except to take you back where you belong," I said. "We don't care to be bothered with you."

"You hold me rather cheaply," he said.

"Very," I replied.

The return of Albert was an easy matter.
I met a colonel, to whom I delivered him and
also the message from our council. The colonel
did not seem to know of Albert's intended mission, for the message puzzled him. I offered
no explanations, leaving him to exaggerate it
or diminish it in the transmission as he pleased.

When I turned away after our brief colloquy,
I saw Kate Van Auken, which was what I had
hoped for when I asked the privilege of bringing Albert back. Her paleness and look of care
had increased, but again I was compelled to
confess to myself that her appearance did not
suffer by it. There was no change in her
spirit.

"Have you become envoy extraordinary
and minister plenipotentiary between the two
camps, Dick?" she asked in a tone that seemed
to me to be touched slightly with irony.

"Perhaps," I replied; "I have merely brought
your brother back to you again, Mistress
Catherine."

"We are grateful."

"This makes twice I've saved him for you,"
I said, "and I've brought Chudleigh back to
you once. I want to say that if you have any

other relatives and friends who need taking care
of, will you kindly send for me?"

"You have done much for us," she said.
"There is no denying it."

"Perhaps I have," I said modestly. "When
I presented Chudleigh to you, you called me a
fool. I suppose you are willing now to take it
back."

"I was most impolite, I know, and I'm
sorry——"

"Oh, you take it back, then?"

"I'm sorry that I have to regret the expression, for, Dick, that is what you are."

There was the faintest suspicion of a smile
on her face, and I could not become quite as
angry as I did on the first occasion. But she
showed no inclination to take the harsh word
back, and perforce I left very much dissatis-
fied.

When I returned to our camp I found much
activity prevailing. It seemed to be the intention of our leaders to close in and seize the
prize without further delay. No attack was to
be made upon Burgoyne's camp, but the circle
of fire which closed him in became broader
and pressed tighter. The number of sharp-

shooters was doubled, and there was scarce a point in the circumference of Burgoyne's camp which they could not reach with their rifle balls, while the British could not attempt repayment without exposing themselves to destruction. Yet they held out, and we did not refuse them praise for their bravery and tenacity.

The morning after my return I said to Whitestone that I gave the British only three days longer. Whitestone shook his head.

" Maybe," he said, " and maybe not so long. They've been cut off at a new point."

I asked him what he meant.

" Why, the British are dying of thirst," he said. " They are in plain sight of the Hudson— in some places they are not more than a few yards from it—but our sharpshooters have crept up till they can sweep all the space between the British camp and the river. The British can't get water unless they cross that strip of ground, and every man that's tried to cross it has been killed."

I shuddered. I could not help it. This was war—war of the kind that wins, but I did not like it. Yet, despite my dislike, I was to take part in it, and that very soon. It was known

that I was expert with the rifle, and I was ordered to choose a good weapon and join a small
detachment that lay on a hill commanding the
narrowest bit of ground between the British
camp and the river. About a dozen of us were
there, and I was not at all surprised to find
Whitestone among the number. It seemed
that if I went anywhere and he didn't go too,
it was because he was there already.

"I don't like this, Whitestone. I don't
like it a bit," I said discontentedly.

"You can shoot into the air," he said, "and
it won't be any harm. There are plenty of
others who will shoot to kill."

I could see that Whitestone was right about
the others. Most of them were from the
mountains of Virginia and Pennsylvania, backwoodsmen and trained Indian fighters, who
thought it right to shoot an enemy from ambush. In truth this was a sort of business they
rather enjoyed, as it was directly in their line.

As I held some official rank I was in a certain sense above the others, though I was not
their commander, each man knowing well what
he was about and doing what he chose, which
was to shoot plump at the first human being

that appeared on the dead line. A thin, active Virginian had climbed a tree in order to get a better aim, and shot with deadly effect from its boughs.

I sat down behind a clump of earth and examined my rifle.

"Look across there," said Whitestone, pointing to the open space.

I did so, and for the second time that day I shuddered. Prone upon the ground were three bodies in the well-known English uniform. A pail lay beside one of them. I knew without the telling of it that those men had fallen in their attempt to reach the water which flowed by—millions and millions of gallons— just out of reach.

"It's rather dull now; nobody's tried to pass the dead line for an hour," said Bucks, a man from the mountains of western Pennsylvania, with a face of copper like an Indian's.

"Did any one succeed in passing?" I asked.

"Pass!" said Bucks, laughing. "What do you reckon we're here for? No sirree! The river is just as full as ever."

There was an unpleasant ring in the man's voice which gave me a further distaste for the work in hand. Our position was well adapted to our task. The hill was broken with low outcroppings of stone and small ridges. So long as we exercised moderate caution we could aim and shoot in comparative safety. Bucks spoke my thoughts when he said:

" It's just like shooting deer at a salt lick."

But the dullness continued. Those red-clad bodies, two of them with their faces upturned to the sun, were a terrible warning to the others not to make the trial. Two of our men, finding time heavy, produced a worn pack of cards and began to play old sledge, their rifles lying beside them.

The waters of the broad river glittered in the sun. Now and then a fish leaped up and shot back like a flash, leaving the bubbles to tell where he had gone. The spatter of musketry around the circle of the British camp had become so much a habit that one noticed it only when it ceased for the time. The white rings of smoke from the burnt powder floated away, peaceful little clouds, and, like patches of snow against the blue sky, helped out the beauty of an early autumn day.

All of us were silent except the two men

19

playing cards. I half closed my eyes, for the sun
was bright and the air was warm, and gave myself up to lazy, vague thought. I was very
glad that we had nothing to do, and even should
the time to act come, I resolved that I would
follow Whitestone's hint.

The two men playing cards became absorbed in the game. One threw down a card
and uttered a cry of triumph.

" Caught your Jack! "

" All right," said the other; " it's only two
for you, your low, Jack against my high, game.
I'm even with you."

I became interested. I was lying on my
back with my head on a soft bunch of turf. I
raised up a little that I might see these players,
who could forget such a business as theirs in
a game of cards. Their faces were sharp and
eager, and when they picked up the cards I
could tell by their expression whether they
were good or bad.

" Four and four," said one, " and this hand
settles the business. Five's the game."

The other began to deal the cards, but a
rifle was fired so close to my ear that the sound
was that of a cannon. The echo ceasing, I

heard Bucks and the man in the tree swearing profusely at each other.

"He's mine, I tell you!" said Bucks.

"It was my bullet that did it!" said the man in the tree with equal emphasis.

"I guess it was both of you," put in White-stone. "You fired so close together I heard only one shot, but I reckon both bullets counted."

This seemed to pacify them. I looked over the little ridge of earth before us, and saw a fourth red-clad body lying on the greensward near the river. It was as still as the others.

"He made a dash for the water," said White-stone, who caught my eye, "but the lead over-took him before he was halfway."

The two men put aside their cards, business being resumed; but after this attempt we lay idle a long time. Bucks, who had an infernal zeal, never took his eyes off the greensward save to look at the priming of his gun.

"I could hit the mark at least twenty yards farther than that," he said to me confidently.

Noon came, and I hoped I would be relieved of this duty, but it was not so. It seemed that it would be an all-day task. The men took some bread and cold meat from their pouches and we ate. When the last crumb fell, a man appeared at the edge of the greensward and held up his hands. Bucks's finger was already on the trigger of his gun, but I made him stop. The man's gesture meant something, and, moreover, I saw that he was unarmed. I called also to the Virginian in the tree to hold his fire.

I thought I knew the meaning of the pantomime. I took my rifle and turned the muzzle of it to the earth so conspicuously that the Englishman, who was holding up his hands, could not fail to see. When he saw, he advanced boldly, and laying hold of one of the bodies dragged it away. He returned for a second, and a third, and then a fourth, and when he had taken the last he did not come back again.

" That's a good job well done! " I said with much relief when the last of the fallen men had been taken away. It was much pleasanter to look at the greensward now, since there was no red spot upon it. I said to Whitestone that I thought the English would not make the trial again.

" They will," he replied. " They must have

water, and maybe they don't know even yet what kind of riflemen we have."

Whitestone was right. In a half hour a man appeared protecting his body with a heavy board as long as himself. He moved with slowness and awkwardness, but two or three bullets fired into the board seemed to make no impression.

"At any rate, if he reaches the river and gets back all right it's too slow a way to slake the thirst of many," said Whitestone in the tone of a philosopher.

Bucks's face puffed out with anger.

"They mustn't get a drop!" he said with the freedom of a backwoodsman. "We're to keep 'em from it; that's what we're here for."

The man looked fierce in his wrath and I did not reprove him, for after all he was right, though not very polite.

The man in the tree fired, and a tiny patch of red cloth flew into the air. The bullet had cut his clothes, but it could not reach the man, who continued to shamble behind his board toward the river.

"I'm afraid we won't be able to stop him," I said to Bucks.

Bucks had crawled to the edge of the hill and was watching with the ferocity and rancor of a savage for a chance to shoot. Often I think that these men who live out in the forests among the savages learn to share their nature.

I could not see because of the board, but I guessed that the man carried a bucket, or pail, in one hand. In truth I was right, for presently a corner of the pail appeared, and it was struck instantly by a bullet from the rifle of the man in the tree.

"At any rate, we've sprung a leak in his pail for him," said Whitestone.

I began to take much interest in the matter. Not intending it, I felt like a hunter in pursuit of a wary animal. My scruples were forgotten for the moment. I found myself sighting along the barrel of my rifle seeking a shot. The Englishman had ceased for me to be a human being like myself. I caught a glimpse of a red-coat sleeve at the edge of the board and would have fired, but as my finger touched the trigger it disappeared and I held back. Whitestone was at my shoulder, the same eagerness showing on his face. The man in the tree had squirmed like a snake far out on the bough, and was seeking for a shot over the top of the board.

The Englishman trailed himself and his protecting board along, and was within a yard of the water. Over the earthwork at the edge of the British camp the men were watching him. His friends were as eager for his success as we were to slay him. It was a rivalry that incited in us a stronger desire to reach him with the lead. In such a competition a man's life becomes a very small pawn. For us the Englishmen had become a target, and nothing more.

Bucks was the most eager of us. He showed his teeth like a wolf.

The Englishman reached the water and stooped over to fill his pail. Bending, he forgot himself and thrust his head beyond the board. With a quickness that I have never seen surpassed, Bucks threw up his rifle and fired. The Englishman fell into the water as dead as a stone, and, his board and his pail falling too, floated off down the stream.

I uttered a cry of triumph, and then clapped my hand in shame over my mouth. The water pulling at the Englishman's body took it out into the deeper stream, and it too floated away.

The zest of the chase was gone for me in an instant, and I felt only a kind of pitying horror. Never before in my life had I been assigned to work so hateful.

Bucks crawled back all a-grin. I turned my back to him while he received the praise of the man in the tree. It was evident to me that nobody could cross the dead line in the face of such sharpshooters, and I hoped the British saw the fact as well as we.

Our enemies must have been very hard pressed, for after a while another man tried the risk of the greensward. He came out only a few feet, and when a bullet clipped right under his feet he turned and fled back, which drew some words of scorn from Bucks, but which seemed to me to be a very wise and timely act.

I thought that this would be the last trial, but Whitestone again disagreed with me.

" When men are burning up with thirst and see a river full of water running by, they'll try mighty hard to get to that river," he said.

The sergeant's logic looked good, but for a full hour it failed. I felt sleepy, again, but was aroused by the man in the tree dropping some twigs, one of which struck me in the face.

"They're going to try it again," he said.

As I have remarked, we could see a small earthwork which the British had thrown up, and whoever tried to pass the dead line would be sure to come from that point. The man in the tree had a better view than we, and I guessed that he saw heads coming over the earthwork.

Among our men was a slight bustle that told of preparation, a last look at the flints, a shoving forward for a better position. I looked at my own rifle, but I resolved that I would not allow zeal to overcome me again. I would remember Whitestone's suggestion and fire into the air, leaving the real work to Bucks and the others, who would be glad enough to do it. I saw the flutter of a garment at the earthwork and some one came over. The man on the bough above me uttered a cry, to which I gave the echo. All the blood in me seemed to rush to my head.

Kate Van Auken, carrying a large bucket in her hand, stepped upon the greensward and walked very calmly toward the river, not once

turning her eyes toward the hill where she
knew the sharpshooters lay. Behind her came
a strapping, bare-armed Englishwoman, who
looked like a corporal's wife, and then four more
women, carrying buckets or pails.

Bucks raised his rifle and began to take aim.
I sprang up and dashed his rifle aside. I am
afraid I swore at him too. I hope I did.

"What are you about, Bucks?" I cried.
"Would you shoot a woman?"

"Mr. Shelby," he replied very coolly,
"we're put here to keep the British from that
water, man or woman. What's a woman's life
to the fate of a whole army? You may outrank
me, but you don't command me in this case,
and I'm going to shoot."

I stooped down and with a sudden movement snatched the gun from his grasp.

"Don't mind it, Bucks," said the man in
the tree; "I'll shoot."

"If you do," I cried, "I'll put a bullet
through you the next moment."

"And if you should chance to miss," said
Whitestone, coming up beside me, "I've a bullet in my gun for the same man."

The man in the tree was no martyr, nor

wanting to be, and he cried out to us that he
would not shoot. In proof of it he took his gun-
stock from his shoulder. The other men did
nothing, waiting upon my movements.

" Bucks," I said, " if I give you your gun, do
you promise not to shoot at those women? "

" Do you take all the responsibility? "

" Certainly."

" Give me my gun. I won't use it."

I handed him his rifle, which he took in silence. I don't think Bucks was a bad man,
merely one borne along by an excess of zeal.
He has thanked me since for restraining him.
The women, Kate still leading them, filled their
buckets and pails at the river and walked back
to the camp with the same calm and even step.
Again and again was this repeated, and many
a fever-burnt throat in the besieged camp must
have been grateful. I felt a glow when I sent a
messenger to our colonel with word of what
I had done and he returned with a full indorse-
ment. How could our officers have done otherwise?

I was sorry I could not get a better view of
Kate Van Auken's face. But she never turned
it our way. Apparently she was ignorant of

our existence, though, of course, it was but a pretense, and she knew that a dozen of the best marksmen in America lay on the hill within easy range of her comrades and herself.

"There's but one thing more for you to do, Mr. Shelby," whispered Whitestone.

"What's that?"

"Save the life of madame, her mother. She's the only one yet unsaved by you."

"I will, Whitestone," I replied, "if I get the chance."

After a while, though late, the women ceased to come for the water. Presently the sun went down and that day's work was done.

My belief that Chudleigh was a very fortunate man was deepening.

CHAPTER XXI.

I rose early the next morning, and my first wish was for duties other than keeping the enemy away from the water. I found Whitestone sitting on his camp blanket and smoking his pipe with an expression of deep-seated content.

" What are we to do to-day? " I asked him, for Whitestone usually knew everything.

" I haven't heard of anything," he replied. " Maybe we'll rest. We deserve it, you and I."

Whitestone has some egotism, though I do not undertake to criticise him for it.

It seemed that he was right, for we were like two men forgotten, which is a pleasant thing sometimes in the military life. Finding that we had nothing else to do, we walked toward the British camp, which, as a matter of course, was the great object of curiosity for all of us, and sat down just within the line of our sharpshooters. The zeal and activity of these gentlemen had relaxed in no particular, and the crackle of their rifles was a most familiar sound in our ears.

We had a good position and could note the distressed look of the British camp. The baggage wagons were drawn up with small reference to convenience and more to defense. The house, the cellar of which I knew to be inhabited by women, children, and severely wounded men, was so torn by cannon balls that the wind had a fair sweep through it in many places. Some of the soldiers walking about seemed to us at the distance to be drooping and dejected. Yet they made resistance, and their skirmishers were replying to ours, though but feebly.

While I was watching the house I saw three or four officers in very brilliant uniforms come out. After a few steps they stopped and stood talking together with what seemed to be great earnestness. These men were generals, I was sure; their uniforms indicated it, and I guessed they had been holding conference. It must be a matter of importance or they would not stop on their way from it to talk again. I directed Whitestone's attention, but he was looking already.

"Something's up," I said. "Maybe they are planning an attack upon us."

"Not likely," he replied. "It may be something altogether different."

I knew what was running through his mind, and I more than half agreed with him.

The generals passed into a large tent, which must have been that of Burgoyne himself; but in a minute or two an officer came and took his way toward our camp. He was a tall, fine fellow, rather young, and bore himself with much dignity. Of a certainty he had on his finest uniform, for he was dressed as if for the eye of woman. His epaulets and his buttons flashed back the sun's rays, and his coat was a blaze of scarlet.

The officer drew the attention of other eyes than Whitestone's and mine. In the British camp they seemed to know what he was about, or guessed it. I could see the people drawing together in groups and looking at him, and then speaking to each other, which always indicates great interest. An officer with gray hair whom he passed looked after him, and then covered his face with his hands.

The officer came on with a steady and regular step to the earthwork, where he paused for a moment.

"It may be," said Whitestone, "that you and I were the first to see the beginning of a great event."

The officer stepped upon the earthwork, raising a piece of white cloth in his hand. The fire of the sharpshooters ceased with such suddenness that my ear, accustomed to the sound, was startled at the lack of it.

"I think you've guessed right," I said to Whitestone.

He made no reply, but drew a deep breath at his pipe stem, and then let the smoke escape in a long white curl.

Some of the sharpshooters stepped from covert and looked curiously at the approaching officer.

"Whitestone," I said, "since there is no committee of reception, let us make ourselves one."

He took his pipe from his mouth and followed me. The murmur of the camps, the sound made by the voices of many men, increased. The officer came rapidly. Whitestone and I walked very slowly. He saw us, and, noting my subaltern's uniform, took me for one dispatched to meet him.

When he came very near I saw that his face was frozen into the haughty expression of a man who wishes to conceal mortification. He said at once that he wished to see our commander in chief, and without question Whitestone and I took him to our colonel, who formed his escort to the tent of our commander in chief. Then we returned to our former place near the outposts.

"How long do you think it will take to arrange it?" I asked Whitestone.

"A day or two, at least," he said. "The British will talk with as long a tongue as they can, hoping that Clinton may come yet, and, even if he don't, there will be many things to settle."

Whitestone was right, as he so often was. The generals soon met to talk, and we subalterns and soldiers relaxed. The rifles were put to rest, and I learned how little we hate our enemies sometimes. I saw one of our senti-

20

nels giving tobacco to a British sentinel, and
they were swapping news over a log. Some
officers sent in medicines for the wounded. No
longer having fear of bullets, I walked up to
the British outworks and looked over them into
the camp. A Hessian sentinel shook his gun
at me and growled something in his throaty
tongue. I laughed at him, and he put his gun
back on his shoulder. I strolled on, and some
one hailed me with a familiar voice. It was Albert Van Auken.

"Hello, Dick!" said he. "Have you folks
surrendered yet? How long are these preliminaries to last?"

He was looking quite fresh and gay, and, if
the truth be told, I was glad to see him.

"No," I replied, "we have not surrendered
yet, and we may change our minds about it."

"That would be too bad," he replied, "after
all our trouble—after defeating you in battle,
and then hemming you in so thoroughly as we
have done."

"So it would," I said. "Sit down and talk
seriously. Are your mother and sister well?"

"Well enough," he replied, "though badly
frightened by your impertinent cannon balls."

He sat down on a mound of earth thrown up by British spades, and I came quite close to him. Nobody paid any attention to us.

"How goes it with Captain Chudleigh?" I asked.

"Poor Chudleigh!" said Albert. "He's lying in the cellar over there, with a ball through his shoulder sent by one of your infernal sharp-shooters."

"Is it bad?" I asked.

"Yes, very," he replied. "He may live, or he may die. Kate's nursing him."

Well, at any rate, I thought, Chudleigh is fortunate in his nurse; there would have been no such luck for me. But I kept the thought to myself.

"Albert," I asked, "what did your officers say to you when I brought you back?"

"Dick," he replied, "let's take an oath of secrecy on that point even from each other."

For his part he kept the oath.

I could not withhold one more gibe.

"Albert," I asked, "what do you Tories say now to the capture of an entire British army by us ragged Continentals?"

He flushed very red.

" You haven't done it," he replied. " Clinton will come yet."

We talked a little further, and then he went
back into his camp.

The talk of the generals lasted all that day
and the next, and was still of spirit and endurance on the third. We soldiers and subalterns,
having little to do, cultivated the acquaintance
of the enemy whom we had fought so long.
Some very lively conversations were carried on
across the earthworks, though, of course, we
never went into their camp, nor did they come
into ours.

On the third day, when I turned away after
exchanging some civilities with a very courteous Englishman, I met a common-looking man
whose uniform was a Continental coat, dis-
tressingly ragged and faded, the remainder of
his costume being of gray homespun. He
nodded as he passed me, and strolled very
close to the British lines. In fact, he went
so close that he seemed to me to intend
going in. Thinking he was an ignorant fellow who might get into trouble by such an
act, I hailed him and demanded where he was
going.

He came back, and laughed in a sheepish way.

"I thought it was no harm," he said.

"I have no doubt you meant none," I said, "but you must not go into their camp."

He bowed very humbly and walked away. His submission so ready and easy attracted my notice, for our soldiers were of a somewhat independent character. I watched him, and noticed that he walked in the swift, direct manner of a man who knows exactly where he is going. Being a bit curious, and having nothing else in particular to do, I followed him at a convenient distance.

He moved three or four hundred yards around the circle of our camp until he came to a place beyond sight of that at which I had stood when I hailed him. The same freedom and ease of communication between the two armies prevailed there.

My man sauntered up in the most careless way, looking about him in the inquisitive fashion of a rustic soldier; but I noted that his general course, however much it zigzagged, was toward the British. I came up much closer. He was within a yard of the British lines and our men were giving him no heed. I felt sure that in a few moments more, if no one interfered, he would be in the British camp. I stepped forward and called to him.

He started in a manner that indicated alarm, and, of course, recognized my face, which he had seen scarce two minutes before. I asked him very roughly why he was trying so hard to steal into the British camp.

"It's true," he said, "I was trying to go in there, but I have a good excuse."

I demanded his excuse.

"I have a brother in there, a Tory," he said, "and I've heard that he's wounded. Everybody says Burgoyne will surrender in a few hours, and I thought it no harm to go in and see my brother."

What he said seemed reasonable. I could readily understand his anxiety on his brother's account. He spoke with such an air of sincerity that I had no heart to scold him; so I told him not to make the attempt again, and if the tale that Burgoyne was to surrender in a few hours was true, he would not have long to wait.

Yet I had a small suspicion left, and I decided to humor it. If there was anything wrong about the man he would watch me, I knew, after two such encounters. I wandered back into our camp as if I had nothing on my mind, though I did not lose sight of him. Among crowds of soldiers there I had the advantage of him, for I could see him and he could not see me.

He idled about a while, and then began to move around the circle of our camp inclosing the British camp. I was glad that I had continued to watch him. Either this man was overwhelmingly anxious about his brother, or he had mischief in mind. I followed him, taking care that he should not see me. Thus engaged, I met Whitestone, who told me something, though I did not stop to hold converse with him about it, not wishing to lose my man.

The fellow made a much wider circle than before, and frequently looked behind him; but he stopped at last and began to approach the British line. There was nobody, at least from our army, within thirty or forty yards of him except myself, and by good luck I was able to find some inequalities of the ground which concealed me.

A British sentinel was standing in a lazy

attitude, and my man approached and hailed him in a friendly manner. The Englishman replied in the same tone.

" Can I go in there? " asked the man, pointing to the British camp.

" You can go in," replied the sentinel with some humor, " but you can't come out again."

" I don't want to come out again," replied the man.

" You chose a curious time to desert," said the sentinel with a sneer, " but it's none of my business."

The man was about to enter, but I stepped forward quickly, drawing my pistol as I did so. He saw me and raised his hand, as if he too would draw a weapon, but I had him under the muzzle of my pistol and threatened to shoot him if he made resistance. Thereupon he played the part of wisdom and was quiet.

" I will take care of this deserter," I said to the English sentinel.

" I told him it was none of my business, and I tell you the same," the sentinel said, shrugging his shoulders. " We're not fighting now. Only don't shoot the poor devil."

"March!" I said to the man, still covering him with my pistol.

"Where?" he asked.

"To the little clump of woods yonder," I said. "I have something to say to you."

The fellow had hard, strong features, and his countenance did not fall.

He wheeled about and marched toward the wood. I followed close behind, the pistol in my hand. I had chosen my course with my eyes open. Our people were not near, and we reached the trees without interruption or notice. In their shelter the man turned about.

"Well, what do you want?" he asked in sullen, obstinate tones.

"Your papers," I said; "the message you were trying to carry into the British camp."

"I have no papers; I was not trying to carry anything into the British camp," he replied, edging a little closer.

"Keep off!" I said, foreseeing his intent. "If you come an inch nearer I will put a pistol ball through you. Stand farther away!"

He stepped back.

"Now give me that letter, or whatever you have," I said. "It is useless to deny that you

have something. If you don't give it to me,
I will take you into the camp and have you
stripped and searched by the soldiers. It will
be better for you to do as I say."

Evidently he believed me, for he thrust his
hand inside his waistcoat and pulled out a
crumpled letter, which he handed to me. Keeping one eye on him I read the letter with the
other eye, and found I had not been deceived
in my guess. It was from Sir Henry Clinton
to Sir John Burgoyne, telling him to hold out
for certain rescue. Sir Henry said he was within
a short distance of Albany with a strong force,
and expected to join Sir John soon and help
him crush all the rebel forces.

"This is important," I said.

"Very," said the man.

"It might have changed the fate of the campaign had you reached General Burgoyne with
it," I said.

"Undoubtedly it would have done so," he
replied.

"Well, it wouldn't."

"That is a matter of opinion."

"Not at all."

"I don't understand you."

"The campaign is ended. Burgoyne surrendered a half hour ago."

Which was true, for Whitestone, with his
skill in finding out things before other people,
had told me.

"I'm very sorry," said the man in tones of
sharp disappointment.

"I'm not," I said.

"What do you mean to have done with
me?" he asked—"hanging, or shooting?"

I did not admire the man, but I respected
his courage.

"Neither," I replied. "You can't do any
harm now. Be off!"

He looked surprised, but he thanked me
and walked away.

It was unmilitary, but it has always been
approved by my conscience, for which I alone
am responsible.

CHAPTER XXII.

CAPITULATIONS.

I stood with Whitestone and saw the British lay down their arms, and, of all the things I saw on that great day, an English officer with the tears dropping down his face impressed me most.

We were not allowed to exult over our enemies, nor did we wish it; but I will not deny that we felt a great and exhilarating triumph. Before the war these Englishmen had denied to us the possession of courage and endurance as great as theirs. They had called us the degenerate descendants of Englishmen, and one of their own generals, who had served with us in the great French and Indian war, and who should have known better, had boasted that with five thousand men he could march from one end of the colonies to the other. Now, more than five thousand of their picked men were laying down their arms to us, and as many more had fallen, or been taken on their way from Canada to Saratoga.

I repeat that all these things—the taunts and revilings of the English, who should have been the last to cheapen us—had caused much bitterness in our hearts, and I assert again that our exultation, repressed though it was, had full warrant. Even now I feel this bitterness sometimes, though I try to restrain it, for the great English race is still the great English race, chastened and better than it was then, I hope and believe.

Remembering all these things, I say that we behaved well on that day, and our enemies, so long as they told the truth, could find no fault with us.

There was a broad meadow down by the river-side, and the British, company after company, filed into this meadow, laid down their arms, and then marched, prisoners, into our lines. Our army was not drawn up that it might look on, yet Whitestone and I stood where we could see.

Some women, weary and worn by suspense and long watches, came across the meadow,

but Kate Van Auken was not among them. I
guessed that she was by the side of the wounded
Chudleigh. When the last company was laying
down its arms, I slipped away from Whitestone
and entered the British camp.

I found Chudleigh in a tent, where they had
moved him from the cellar that he might get
the fresher air. Kate, her mother, and an English surgeon were there. The surgeon had just
fastened some fresh bandages over the wound.
Chudleigh was stronger and better than I had
expected to find him. He even held out his hand
to me with the smile of one who has met an
enemy and respects him.

" I will be all right soon, Shelby," he said,
" so the doctor tells me, if you rebels know how
to treat a wounded prisoner well."

" In a month Captain Chudleigh will be as
well as he ever was," said the surgeon.

I was very glad on Kate's account. Presently she walked out of the tent, and I followed
her.

" Kate," I asked, " when will the marriage
occur? "

" What marriage? " she asked very sharply.

" Yours and Chudleigh's."

" Never! "

" What! " I exclaimed in surprise. " Are you not going to marry Chudleigh? "

" No."

" Are you not betrothed to him? "

" No. That was my mother's plan for me."

" Are you not in love with him? "

" No."

I was silent a moment.

" Kate," I asked, " what does this mean? "

" Dick," she said, " I have told you twice what you are."

Her cheeks were all roses.

" Kate," I said, " love me."

" I will not! "

" Be my betrothed? "

" I will not! "

" Marry me? "

" I will not! "

Which refusals she made with great emphasis—every one of which she took back.

She was a woman.

THE END.

www.ingramcontent.com/pod-product-compliance
Lightning Source LLC
Chambersburg PA
CBHW020241290326
41929CB00045B/1191